Naturally Powered
Old Time Toys

NATURALLY POWERED OLD TIME TOYS

How to Make Sun Yachts, Sail Cars, a Monkey on a String, and Other Moving Toys

Marjorie Henderson and Elizabeth Wilkinson

with crafts illustrated by Martha Weston
and photographed by Tom Liden

J. B. Lippincott Company/Philadelphia and New York

This book was developed and prepared for publication under the
direction of James and Carolyn Robertson at the Yolla Bolly Press,
Covelo, California, during the winter and spring of 1977-78.
Editorial assistant: Jay Stewart. Typesetting: Gene Floyd.
Layout: Diana Fairbanks. Production assistants: Joyca Cunnan
and Loren Fisher.

U.S. Library of Congress Cataloging in Publication Data

Henderson, Marjorie.
    Naturally powered old time toys: how to make
sun yachts, sail cars, a monkey on a string, and
other moving toys.
    1. Toy making—Amateurs' manuals. I. Wilkinson,
Elizabeth, birth date   joint author. II. Title.
TT174.H45   745.59'2   78-8556
ISBN-0-397-01308-6
ISBN-0-397-01316-7 (pbk.)

Contents

Toymakers' Introduction

One of the happiest of occupations, whether you are a child or a grownup, is making toys. We would rather build toys than write about them, but two women of mature years and presumed good sense need some kind of excuse for flying kites and playing with tin steamboats, which is what we do to test out our models. Our activities occasionally require the space of a public park, and when we encounter stares and raised eyebrows, we are glad to have the reasonable explanation of "a book in progress."

Still, why anyone should need an excuse for building toys, we can't imagine. What better reason could there be than that it's fun? It's not only fun but one of the most creative pastimes. We have, over the years, experimented with all kinds of more formal adult crafts from needlepoint to woodworking. Yet none of these has the scope or the wide open possibilities for creativity that toymaking does.

Building moving toys — toys that do something — is a fascinating pursuit. It can be an inexpensive hobby, an art form, an outlet for a frustrated inventor, a sentimental trip for the nostalgic, or, most especially, a good time for parents and children. Since nobody takes a toy very seriously, there need be no restraints on how it looks or how it is made. There is no "right way," so the builder is totally free to try the imaginative, the preposterous, the downright goofy way. And try them all we have — with some enchanting and occasionally hilarious results.

We found the designs for these toys in books and magazines, mostly from the nineteenth century. While our initial interest was historical, the longer we worked with them, the more enthusiastic we became about them just as playthings. On first reading about them, we doubted the practicality of the designs. They had a delightful Rube Goldberg quality, but we couldn't believe they would perform as advertised. Victorian writers were long on glowing descriptions but short on directions. We had a happy surprise finding that, with a bit of tinkering, the toys worked very well indeed. Tinkering is basic to moving toys and part of the fun. Success often depends on adding a tiny bit of ballast or bending a wire to a slightly different angle. We learned to experiment freely — and so can you.

We had a wonderful time with our experimentations and found it impossible to resist the urge to make wilder and more wonderful versions. Steamboats became a positive addiction; for weeks we soldered, sailed, and sank a variety of exotic vessels. The house was soon full of odd contraptions: regattas of paper sailboats spinning in the windows, tiny machines pumping their walking beams in sunny corners, sinks full of boats of all descriptions, and in the kitchen, half a dozen steam boilers hissing and spitting — a mad inventor's paradise.

Our steamboat mania hit at the most inconvenient time possible, in the middle of a record drought. However, as the water shortage became acute, we prided ourselves on being able to recycle water three times: for washing, for boat testing, and then for watering the garden.

The antique appearance of these toys is only part of their charm. For us, a chief attraction is the ingenious use of natural forces to make the toys work. Not a battery in the lot! They run on sunlight and wind, water and sand. The most complicated require a homemade alcohol burner, and the simplest, a few hairbrush bristles or a rubber band. An easy and wonderful way to begin learning about simple physics and natural energy.

None of these creations are hard to build. They require more patience than skill. Most are highly adaptable and can be made either complicated or simple, to suit the tastes and ability of the toymaker. We found it most enjoyable to work as a team. When one of us ran out of energy or ideas, the other would automatically shift into gear and take over. A child and parent team would be a most productive toy-building partnership, having a good mix of fresh enthusiasm and practical know-how.

You will need a few tools but nothing unusual or expensive. Sometimes a vise might make things easier, even though it isn't specifically mentioned. The most elaborate — and one of the most intriguing to use — is a soldering iron. The materials needed to make the toys are equally basic: wood, tin, wire, and cardboard. Most can be scrounged easily. Some are simply recycled household items. The few supplies that must be bought are inexpensive and easily found in hardware, lumber, hobby, art supply, and even grocery stores. An excellent and interesting place to look for wood is the dump pile of a cabinetmaker's shop, if you can get permission to go through it. If something special is needed, we've included a note about where to get it in the tools and materials list. The lumber sizes we've given are the standard ones usually found in lumberyards. Don't hesitate to substitute if you have materials on hand that you think will work. The things we specify are those we used with success, but there is always another way.

On first sight, some of these projects may look discouragingly complicated. They aren't. We have given exact step-by-step instructions and plenty of diagrams for any tricky parts and, wherever possible, full scale patterns. There is nothing in this book that you can't do and very probably improve upon. Some things will take longer to build than others, but that does not necessarily mean that they are any harder to build. You might cut, assemble, and be playing with a String Climber in the space of an hour, while the Paper Yacht would require about five hours of work over a span of several days, allowing for drying time. Yet each step in the individual construction is no more difficult in one toy than in the other.

What is more important is for you to feel free to try out your own ideas and techniques. If you think that you can figure out a better way to make something, try it, and let your inventiveness carry you where it will. Most important, of course, and our hope is that you enjoy yourselves, as we did, making and playing with these clever, old-time toys.

PART ONE

SUN AND HEAT POWERED TOYS

Hot Air Put to Good Use

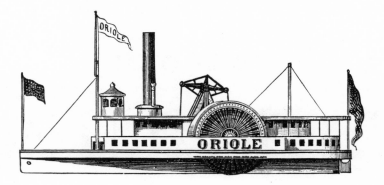

Solar energy seems like such a new idea, but of course it isn't. Man has always recognized the power of the sun and primitive peoples have worshipped the sun as a god. The first preserved food was sun dried, and the earliest pottery was of sun dried clay; but until recent times, the only really practical sun tool that evolved was the burning glass, or lens, which concentrated the rays of the sun at one point to start a fire. This idea was used in ingenious ways, from the noon cannon that fired automatically — it had a lens arranged so that the noon sun would light a fuse and set off a gunpowder charge — to Lavoisier's eighteenth-century solar furnace that used two giant lenses and reached temperatures approaching two thousand degrees Fahrenheit.

Since so little modern-day use has been made of the sun's energy, we were surprised and intrigued to find that sun-powered toys had been designed at the beginning of this century. These toys use the simplest kind of sun power — heat. This is the same form of energy that helps birds to soar and sends sailplanes climbing the sky in thermals, or rising columns of air, created by the heat of the sun.

One of the most basic of scientific facts is that hot air rises, whether it is heated by the sun or by a candle. The simple floating paper toys we describe are an easy and amusing way to demonstrate this principle. Another popular nineteenth-century toy was the hot air balloon. These were tissue paper models ranging up to six feet in height and were an outgrowth of the ballooning craze that began in the eighteenth century. The boys' books of that period often gave plans for gas as well as hot air balloons. The simplest of these was a bladder filled from an unlit gaslight jet. The more complex had directions for making highly explosive hy-drogen gas using sulfuric acid. None of them gave a word of warning about the potential hazards, and we wonder how many workshops were blown up by young amateur scientists. We remember childhood experiences with "safe" chemistry sets that caused very minor explosions, with no more serious results than a newly papered room covered with nasty green spots. The most persistent memory, however, is that parents take a very dim view of this sort of experiment.

We shouldn't have been surprised at either the sun toys or the hydrogen gas. The late 1800s was a time of great awareness of and enthusiasm for scientific and mechanical experimentation. Almost every toymaking book gave instructions on building some type of steam engine. Little boilers, with their alcohol burners, were just as popular with children and their fathers then as electric trains were to later generations. We give plans for a simplified model of the oldest of steam engines, invented by Heron of Alexandria. It was the prototype for them all. Applications of home-built steam power are many and varied.

One simple steamboat uses a baking powder tin laid on its side. It has a large hole for filling the boiler with water that is closed with a cork and a small hole at the back. When the water boils, steam is driven through the small hole with enough force to propel the boat forward. This sounded good in theory, but in reality it doesn't work very well. A variation on this idea has a narrow metal tube soldered to the small hole and bent to direct the steam underwater. When we tried this, it made grand noises but didn't go very far. A much more successful propellant is the coiled tube that powers our tin steamboat. This uses the principle of convection and works well.

Heating the air in a balloon to test for leaks.

Adding a gondola to the finished balloon.

You didn't have to build a steam engine at home. Ads like this one from the Boy's Own Paper, *November 1896, were common. They offered completed engines as well as parts for assembling your own.*

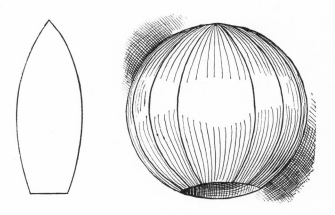

Shape of gores and a design for a tissue paper balloon showing the gores assembled.

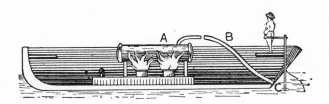

Toy boat with direct steam drive; the metal tube carried the steam underwater and was supposed to send the boat along at a good rate.

A model steamboat in action, but not going anywhere very fast.

A FLOATING CARNIVAL OF CANDLES

Everyone likes to play with fire, and here are some ways to do it without much risk or expense. These toys were first built around 1900 — a time when many homes were still lit by candles and oil lamps, and children grew up using and respecting fire. What makes these projects reasonably safe for today's un-initiated youngsters is that they are all de-signed to float on water: in the bathtub, the fishpond, or a tub in the backyard. If a few of them go up in flames, it's all part of the fun.

Here is an experiment to try before you start any of these projects. Float a piece of regular binder paper in a basin of water. Crumple up some more paper and place it gently on the floating sheet. Add a few wooden matches to the pile and set the wadded paper and matches on fire. You will be interested to see what happens.

Mouse-Go-Round

This is a good candle project for starters. It's so easy to make that you won't really mind if it ends up in the same state as the bonfire experiment. We burned up a few mice before we found out just how close the candles could be placed.

Tools and Materials

Scissors
Tracing paper
Rubber cement or white glue
Marking pens: pink and black
Wrapping paper: brown or white
Construction paper: heavyweight, soft brown or white
Candle stubs: four 1-inch pieces

To Build a Mouse-Go-Round

Cut a 16-inch circle of wrapping paper. Be careful not to crease or curl it. Trace the pat-terns for mouse and tail, and cut four mice and four tails from the construction paper. Be sure not to cut along the fold line. Curl the tails by running them over a scissors blade. Color the eyes, ears, noses, and paws pink. Circle the eyes and draw whiskers in with the black pen. Glue the mice to the wrapping paper circle, as shown, spacing them at even intervals from each other and 1 1/2 inches in from the edge.

Now place the paper circle gently on the sur-face of the water, taking care that no water runs over the edge of the paper. Carefully set a candle stub in front of each mouse's nose and light it. The mice will soon start to revolve. The reason they always go backwards is that they don't want to burn their whiskers.

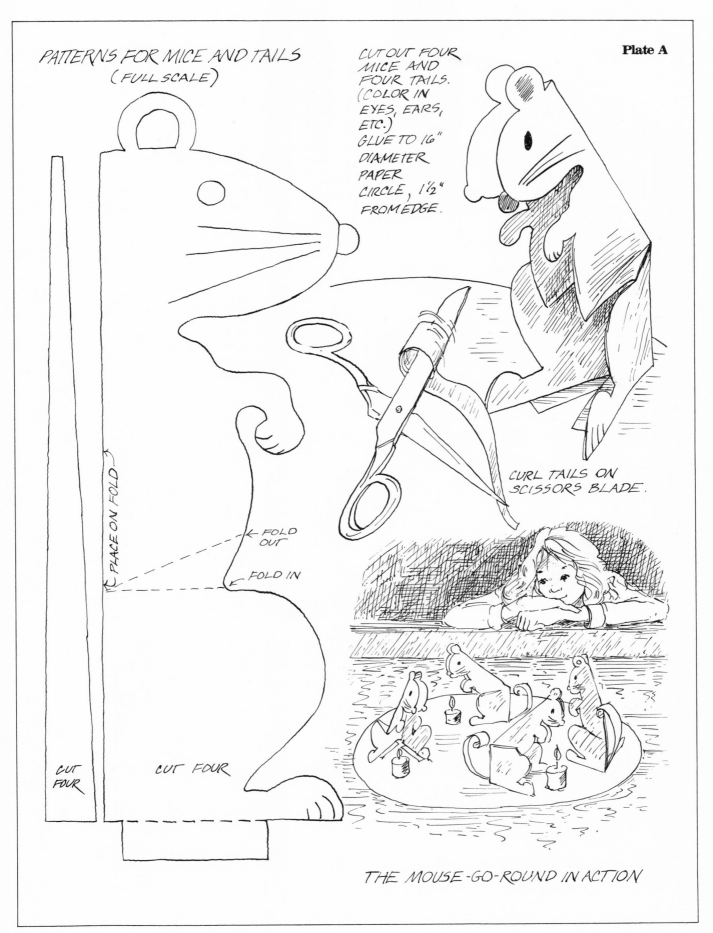

PATTERNS FOR MICE AND TAILS
(FULL SCALE)

CUT OUT FOUR MICE AND FOUR TAILS. (COLOR IN EYES, EARS, ETC.) GLUE TO 16" DIAMETER PAPER CIRCLE, 1½" FROM EDGE.

Plate A

PLACE ON FOLD

← FOLD OUT

← FOLD IN

CURL TAILS ON SCISSORS BLADE.

CUT FOUR

CUT FOUR

THE MOUSE-GO-ROUND IN ACTION

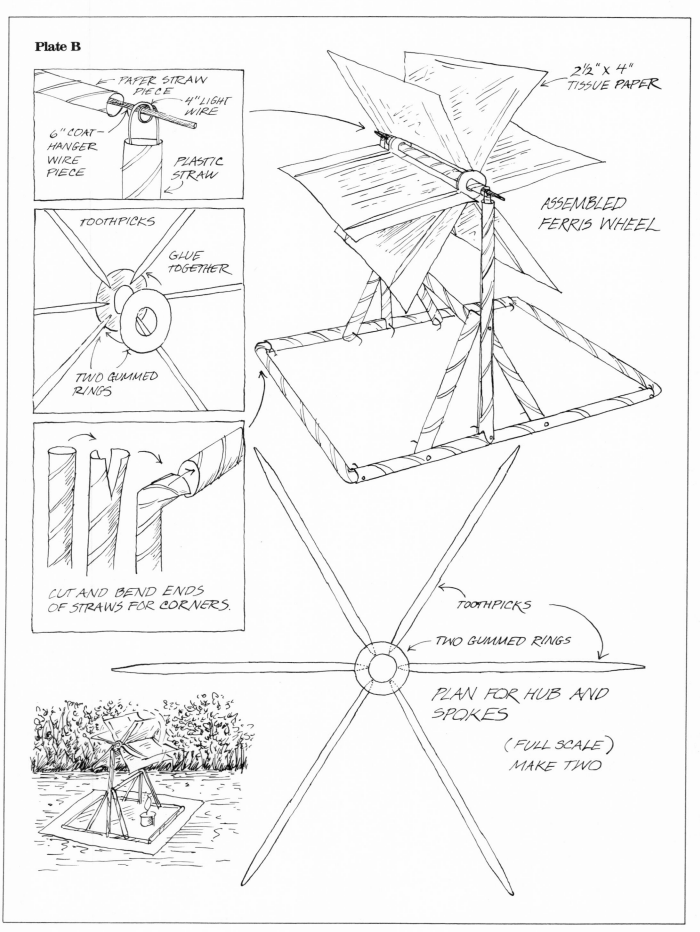

Plate B

PAPER STRAW PIECE

4" LIGHT WIRE

6" COAT-HANGER WIRE PIECE

PLASTIC STRAW

TOOTHPICKS

GLUE TOGETHER

TWO GUMMED RINGS

CUT AND BEND ENDS OF STRAWS FOR CORNERS.

2½" × 4" TISSUE PAPER

ASSEMBLED FERRIS WHEEL

TOOTHPICKS

TWO GUMMED RINGS

PLAN FOR HUB AND SPOKES

(FULL SCALE)
MAKE TWO

Floating Ferris Wheel

The Ferris Wheel is very pretty and dainty, spinning in the candlelight, especially if you make the sails of colored tissue paper. Alternate colors for the best effect. The spokes and hubs must be made with some precision so that each sail catches the heat just at the right moment to turn the wheel.

Tools and Materials

Scissors
Rubber cement
Wire cutters
Wire coat hanger
Wire: 22-gauge
Straight pins
Plastic drinking straws
Round toothpicks
Gummed reinforcement rings: the kind used
  for binder paper
Paper, typing or binder
Tissue paper
Candle stub

To Build a Ferris Wheel

Make two wheel hubs by sandwiching the toothpick ends between double layers of gummed rings. This is most easily done by tracing the full scale plan and taping the toothpicks in place on the plan while you glue the rings to their tips. The spokes must be evenly spaced or the wheel will not turn properly.

Make a rectangular base from four straws to measure about 8 1/2 inches by 5 inches. Split both ends of two of the straws. Bend them at right angles, and insert them into the end of the other two straws as shown. Fix them in place with pins.

The uprights are two straws notched at the bottom so they will fit over the base straws. Pin one to the exact center of each long side of the base. The angled supports are straws bent in half. Cut the crosspiece support from another straw; then pin together, as shown.

Cut a 4-inch length of straw; slip a hub 1 inch in on each end. With the cutting part of the pliers, cut a straight 6-inch wire from the coat hanger to make an axle. Run this through the hub straw. Cut two 4-inch lengths of 22-gauge wire. Twist one tightly around each end of the axle wire leaving both ends long. Push these ends into the tops of the straw uprights.

Cut six 4- by 2 1/2-inch pieces of tissue paper, and glue them to the toothpick spokes. Float a sheet of binder paper on water. Now place the Ferris Wheel carefully on the paper. Gently set a lighted candle stub on one side, as shown.

Enchanted Tower

This revolving tower makes a wonderful party centerpiece to beguile all of us who love fairy tales and castles.

Tools and Materials

Scissors
Felt-tip pens
White glue
Plastic drinking straws
Round toothpicks
Wrapping paper: heavy brown
Tissue paper: a bright color
Typing paper
Candle stubs

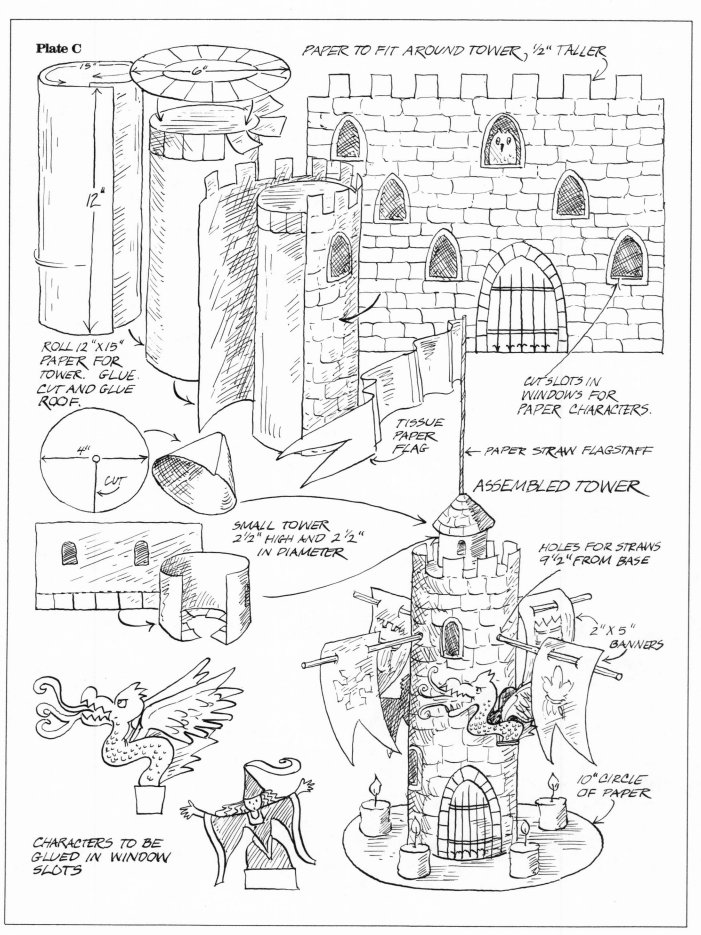

Plate C

15"

6"

12"

PAPER TO FIT AROUND TOWER, ½" TALLER

ROLL 12"X15" PAPER FOR TOWER. GLUE. CUT AND GLUE ROOF.

CUT SLOTS IN WINDOWS FOR PAPER CHARACTERS.

4"

CUT

TISSUE PAPER FLAG

← PAPER STRAW FLAGSTAFF

ASSEMBLED TOWER

SMALL TOWER 2½" HIGH AND 2½" IN DIAMETER

HOLES FOR STRAWS 9½" FROM BASE

2"X5" BANNERS

10" CIRCLE OF PAPER

CHARACTERS TO BE GLUED IN WINDOW SLOTS

base. The sail arms are two straws taped together end to end to make a 16-inch length. Make two of them and push them through the tower, as shown. Cut four 2- by 5-inch banners from typing paper. Cut slits in these and slip them onto the straws. Cut a 10-inch circle of wrapping paper and float it on water. Put the tower in the center with a candle stub beneath each banner. Adjust the banners to about a 30-degree angle, and the whole tower will start to revolve.

Floating Pinwheel

Here is another kind of floating concoction. The folded cardboard base and pivot arrangement can be used for a variety of designs.

Tools and Materials

Scissors
Razor knife
White glue
Straight pin
Plastic drinking straws
Doweling: one piece, 3/8 inch in diameter and 1/2 inch long
Cardboard: lightweight
Cellophane tape: clear
Paper: typing and wrapping
Candle stubs: four or five

To Build an Enchanted Tower

Roll a 12- by 15-inch piece of brown wrapping paper into a tube, 12 inches high and 4 1/2 inches in diameter. Glue it along the seam. Cover one end of this tube with a 6-inch circle of paper, cut and glued as shown. Make a second tube 2 1/2 inches in diameter and 2 1/2 inches high.

Cut another piece of brown paper just large enough to fit around the big tube and 1/2 inch taller. Decorate this paper to look like a medieval tower. Cut out the castellated battlements along the top. Draw and color doors, windows, owls, maidens-in-distress, suitable graffiti, and whatever other fanciful details you like. Glue this around the big tube.

Decorate the small tube in a similar manner and glue it to the roof to make the small tower. Make a pointed roof for it by cutting a 4-inch circle of paper and coloring it a dull red or another suitable color. Slit the circle to the center, form it into a cone, and glue it. Glue a toothpick into the peak for a banner pole. Glue the roof to the small tower. Cut a bright tissue paper banner and attach it to the pole.

Make four 1/4-inch holes at even intervals around the big tower 9 1/2 inches up from the

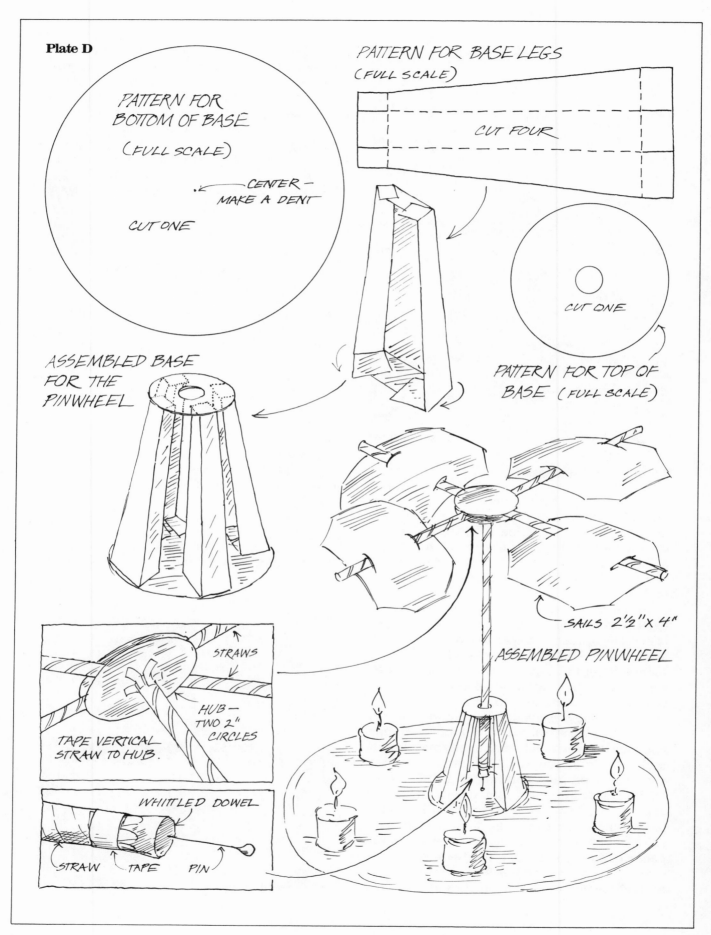

Plate D

PATTERN FOR
BOTTOM OF BASE

(FULL SCALE)

CENTER —
MAKE A DENT

CUT ONE

PATTERN FOR BASE LEGS
(FULL SCALE)

CUT FOUR

CUT ONE

PATTERN FOR TOP OF
BASE (FULL SCALE)

ASSEMBLED BASE
FOR THE
PINWHEEL

SAILS 2'½" X 4"

ASSEMBLED PINWHEEL

STRAWS

HUB —
TWO 2"
CIRCLES

TAPE VERTICAL
STRAW TO HUB.

WHITTLED DOWEL

STRAW   TAPE   PIN

To Build a Pinwheel

Trace the base patterns on lightweight cardboard and cut out. Score with a razor knife along the broken lines on the legs and fold them, as shown. Glue the tabs to each other and to the top and bottom circles, as indicated on the patterns.

To make the pinwheel, cut two 2-inch circles of cardboard. Cut two straws in half and tape them to one of the circles so as to make four evenly spaced spokes. Place the second circle on top and tape it neatly in place taking care not to crush the straws. Center the assembly on the top of a whole straw and tape it securely in place. Cut four 2 1/2- by 4-inch sails from typing paper, slit them as shown, and slip them onto the straw spokes. You can cut the corners of the sails for a more interesting design. Angle all the sails slightly in one direction. Whittle the small piece of dowel down at one end until it will fit into the end of the straw upright like a cork. Push a pin into the center of the dowel until it holds. Don't bend the pin.

Draw the straw upright through the hole in the base. When it is vertical and balanced, mark the point where the pinhead rests. Make a shallow indentation at that point with a blunt pencil point, just enough to keep the pinhead from wandering when the pinwheel turns. Experiment by blowing gently on the sails.

Cut an 8-inch circle of wrapping paper and float it in a basin of water. Place the pinwheel in the center, and surround it with four or five lighted candle stubs, as shown.

Butterfly Circus

This was originally designed as a treetop ornament in the days people still used candles on their Christmas trees. It must have been a wonderful surprise on Christmas Eve to see all of these colorful little butterflies hovering around the top of the tree. You could use this version as a floating table decoration for an Easter or birthday party.

Tools and Materials

Scissors
Razor knife
Needle-nose pliers
Straight pin

White glue
Plastic drinking straws
Doweling: 3/8-inch diameter — one piece, 1/2 inch long
Wrapping paper
Stiff paper: white
Tracing paper
Cardboard: lightweight
Cellophane tape: clear
Wire: 22-gauge
Felt-tip pens: assorted colors
Candle stubs

To Build a Butterfly Circus

Trace and cut out of stiff white paper three or four butterflies of each kind. Decorate them on both sides with felt-tip pens. They may be as fanciful or as realistic as you please. Crease the butterflies up the center and attach 6-inch wires as shown. Tape the wire to the underside of the left wing. Twist the other ends of all the wires neatly together and flatten the twist. Cut two 2-inch circles of cardboard. Center the twist of wire on one of the circles and spread the wires so they are evenly distributed around the circle. Put the second cardboard circle on top and tape them neatly together.

Make the base and pivot straw as you did for the Floating Pinwheel. Center the butterfly assembly at the top of the straw and tape it in place. Arrange the butterflies so that the straw will balance on the base. They must all be flying headed slightly down at much the same angle in order to revolve, but they can be at different heights. Float an 8-inch circle of wrapping paper on water. Put the Butterfly Circus on the paper with several small candles around it.

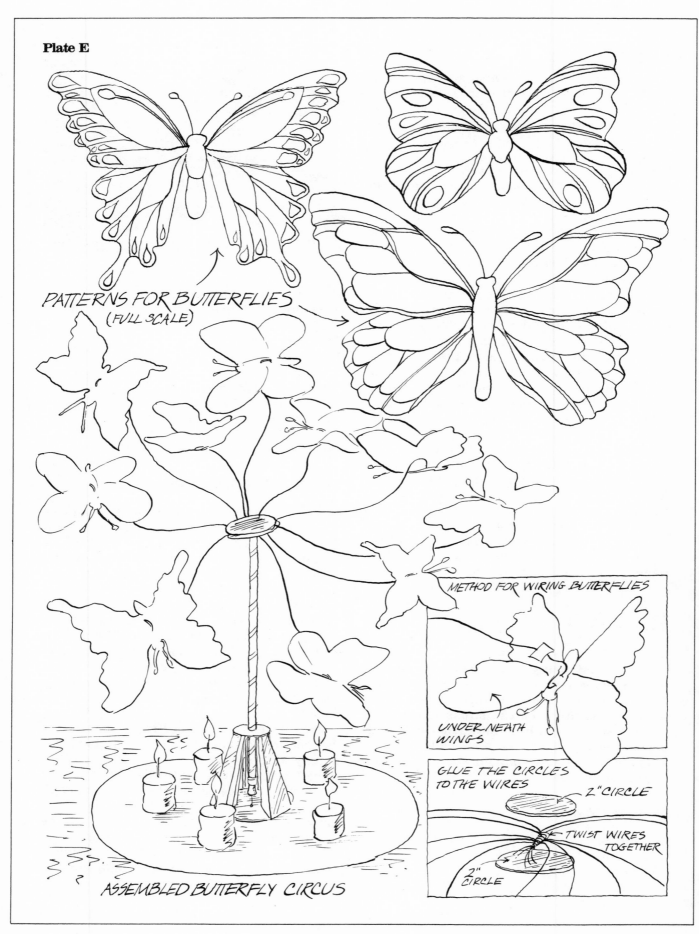

PATTERNS FOR BUTTERFLIES
(FULL SCALE)

METHOD FOR WIRING BUTTERFLIES

UNDERNEATH WINGS

GLUE THE CIRCLES TO THE WIRES

2" CIRCLE

TWIST WIRES TOGETHER

2" CIRCLE

ASSEMBLED BUTTERFLY CIRCUS

SUN YACHTS

Sun Yachts are good toys to build when you are confined indoors on a cold winter's day. You need only the simplest of building materials and a sunny window, for it's the sun that makes them go. Even if the sun isn't shining, the boats will sail briskly around in the slightest draft. It takes no more than the breeze created by someone walking past to set them into motion, and they are very pretty to see.

Tools and Materials

Scissors
Razor knife
Saw
Needle-nose pliers
Paintbrush: small
Drill: with a 1/16-inch and a 3/8-inch bit
Wood: 6 inches by 6 inches by 3/4 inch
Doweling: one piece, 3/8 inch in diameter and 24 inches long
Heavy cardboard: 18 inches by 18 inches
Wire: 18-gauge, 5 feet long
Plastic drinking straws
Straight pins
Thread: button and carpet
Rubber cement or paste
Tissue paper: white, red, and blue
Construction paper: red and blue
Darning needle
Nail: small finishing
Paint: enamel

To Build the Sun Yachts

Cut a ring of heavy cardboard (Plate F) that is 1 inch wide and 16 inches at the outside diameter. Cut a cardboard disk, 1 1/2 inches in diameter. Divide the ring and the disk into eight equal segments with pencil lines. Using scissors, make a hole on each line of the ring and of the disk, 1/4 inch in from the edge. Cut eight 20-inch lengths of thread. Tie one thread through each of the eight holes in the ring. Tie the other ends to the holes in the disk. Each thread must measure exactly 15 inches between the ring and the disk.

Make four holes in the outer edge of the ring, 1/4 inch in from the outer edge, at every other line. Using pliers or wire cutters, cut four pieces of wire, each 13 inches long, and insert one in each hole. These are part of the masts.

Bend the bottom 1 1/2 inch of each wire around the underside of the ring, up over the edge, and finish with a loop around the upright wire, as shown in the diagram. Squeeze the wires tight with pliers so they stand straight up from the ring.

To make the yachts (Plates F and G), trace the sail patterns on white tissue paper and cut out four mainsails and four jibs. (We have used actual boating terms in these instructions. The illustrations show what names go to which part.) Cut out the sail numbers, the 1 and 3 from blue tissue paper and the 2 and 4 from the red. Glue the numbers to the sails. Make masts by cutting two 8 1/2-inch straws in half. Crush one end of each half and insert it into a whole straw to a depth of 1/2 inch. Cut two more straws in half; notch one end of each to form the jaws of the gaffs, as shown. The gaffs are attached to the masts at the points where the mast pieces overlap. Push a straight pin through the jaws of the gaff and the masts to fasten them together. Make four booms of whole straws by cutting jaws at one end. Attach them to the masts 2 inches from the bottom. Bend the ends of the pins at right angles to hold them in. Glue the sails to the mast assemblies so that the bent ends of the pins are concealed. Slip the straw masts over the upright wires.

Cut two hull shapes (Plate H) of red construction paper and two of blue. Glue them, alternating the colors, along the outer edge of the ring so that the bows are 3 1/2 inches in front of the masts. Glue the tacks of the jibs to the bows and the jib heads to the masts, as shown. Bend the masts slightly outward so that the boats are heeling and the booms all swing out. Attach a length of thread to the end of each boom. Sew the other end of this thread to the stern of the boat so that all of the sails are held at the same angle.

To make the stand (Plate H), drill a 3/8-inch hole in the center of the 6-inch square piece of wood. Glue the 24-inch piece of doweling into the hole. You can paint either or both to make a prettier base. Drill a 1/16-inch hole in the top of the dowel. Put a small finishing nail in the hole, point up. Balance the center point of the cardboard disk on the point of the nail so that the ring is suspended evenly. Set the yachts in a sunny window and watch them revolve.

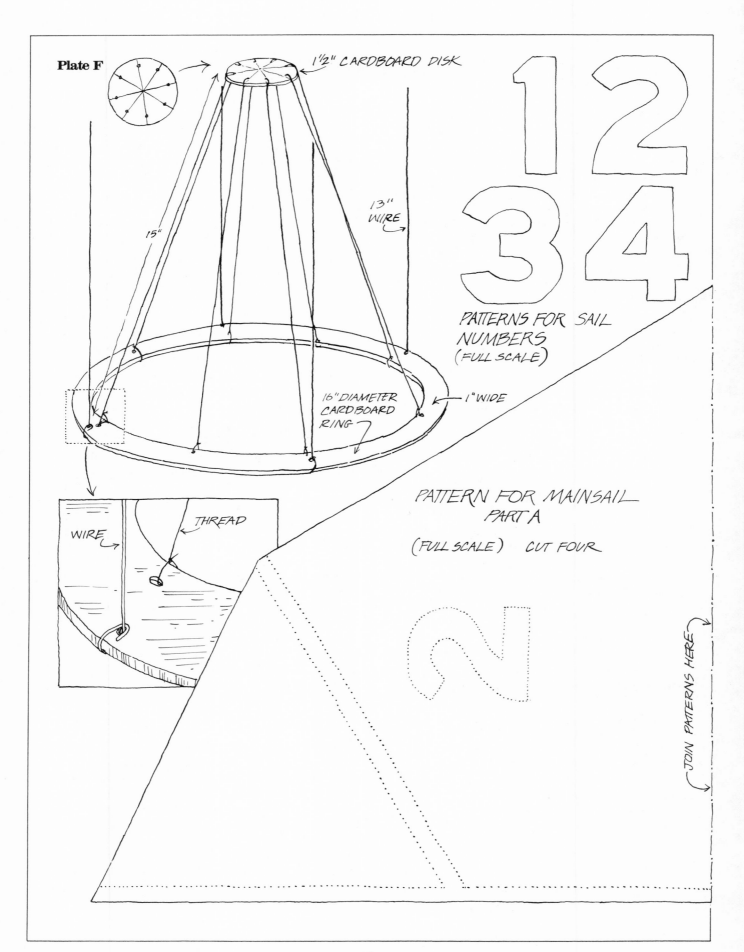

Plate F

1½" CARDBOARD DISK

15"

13" WIRE

1 2 3 4

PATTERNS FOR SAIL NUMBERS (FULL SCALE)

16" DIAMETER CARDBOARD RING

1" WIDE

WIRE

THREAD

PATTERN FOR MAINSAIL PART A

(FULL SCALE)   CUT FOUR

2

JOIN PATTERNS HERE

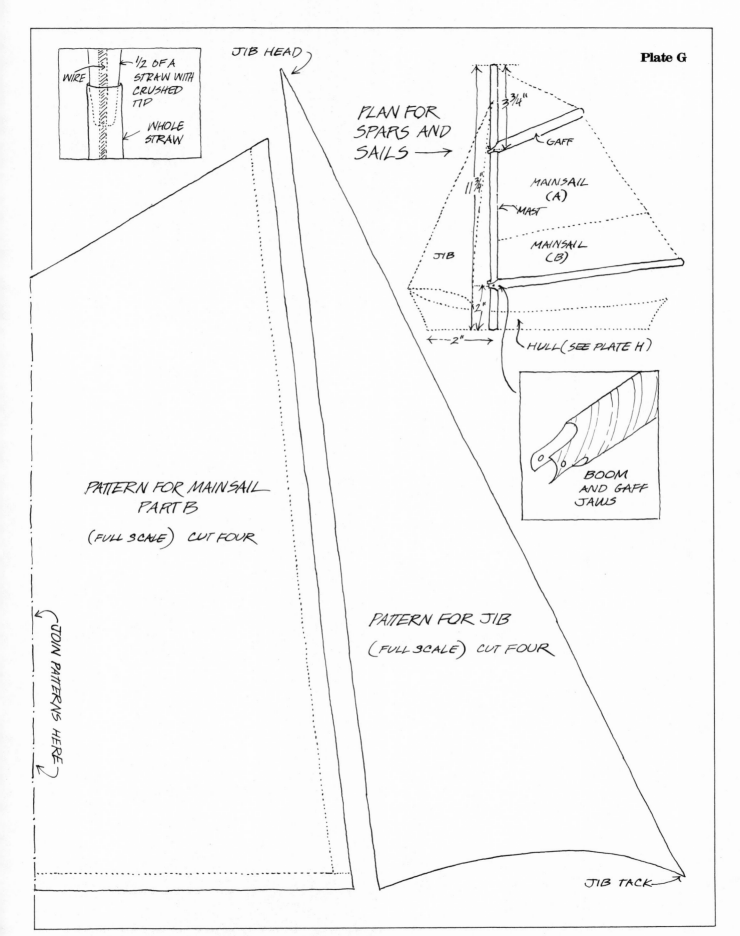

WIRE ½ OF A STRAW WITH CRUSHED TIP

WHOLE STRAW

JIB HEAD

Plate G

PLAN FOR SPARS AND SAILS →

3¾"

GAFF

11¾"

MAINSAIL (A)

MAST

JIB

MAINSAIL (B)

2"

← 2" →

HULL (SEE PLATE H)

BOOM AND GAFF JAWS

PATTERN FOR MAINSAIL PART B

(FULL SCALE) CUT FOUR

JOIN PATTERNS HERE

PATTERN FOR JIB

(FULL SCALE) CUT FOUR

JIB TACK

Plate H

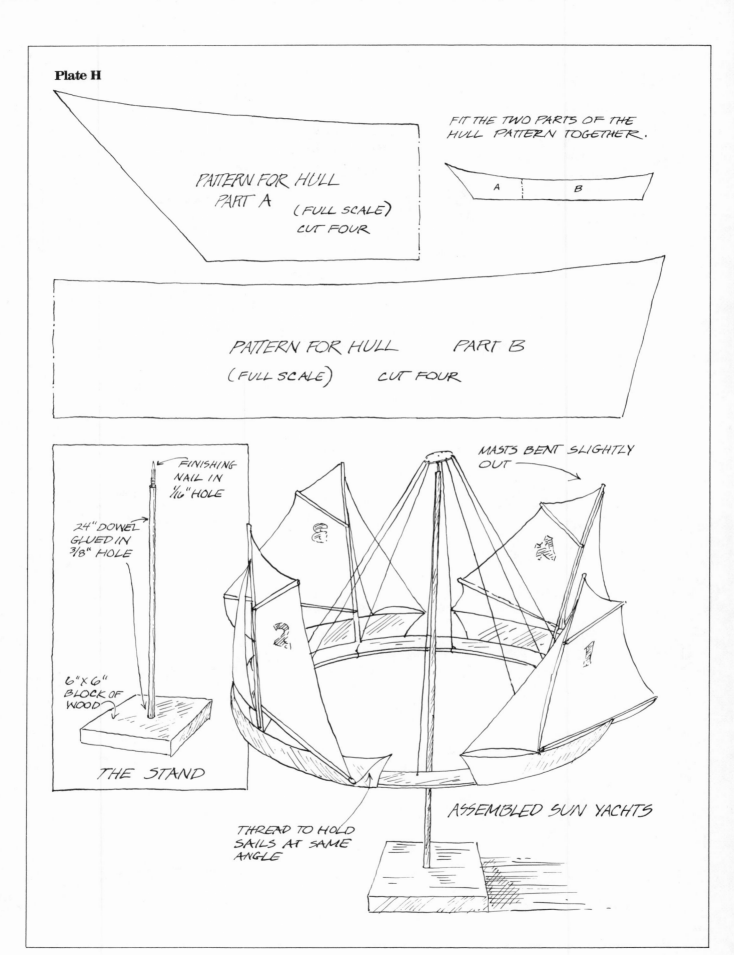

PATTERN FOR HULL
PART A
(FULL SCALE)
CUT FOUR

FIT THE TWO PARTS OF THE
HULL PATTERN TOGETHER.

A   B

PATTERN FOR HULL   PART B
(FULL SCALE)   CUT FOUR

FINISHING
NAIL IN
¹/₁₆" HOLE

24" DOWEL
GLUED IN
³/₈" HOLE

6" X 6"
BLOCK OF
WOOD

THE STAND

MASTS BENT SLIGHTLY
OUT

THREAD TO HOLD
SAILS AT SAME
ANGLE

ASSEMBLED SUN YACHTS

SUNSHINE ENGINE

This toy offers you the ultimate tinkering experience. It's a gadgeteer's delight. The sun sets its sails spinning, and this turns the driving wheel, flywheel, walking beam, and piston. This is a sensitive little contraption, and all of the parts have to be carefully balanced before it will work properly. So if at first you don't suceed, tinker away. You may want to invent an engine of your own, but if you do, keep all of the parts very light in weight.

Tools and Materials

Saw
Metal file
Needle-nose pliers
Hammer
Razor knife
Drill: with a 1/8-inch bit, a 1/4-inch bit, and a 1/16-inch bit
Scissors
Tin snips
Paintbrush: small

White glue
Nails: 1-inch
Carpet tacks
Plywood: one piece, 6 inches by 6 inches by 1/2 inch thick; one piece, 6 inches by 10 inches by 1/2 inch thick
Wood: one piece, 1/2 inch by 1/2 inch by 8 inches; one piece, 3/4 inch by 1/4 inch by 5 inches
Doweling: 1/4-inch diameter — one piece, 14 inches long; two pieces, 10 inches long
Drinking straws: eleven
Thread: one piece of light sewing thread, 20 inches long
Cork: one, 1 1/2 inches in diameter
Straight pins
Lightweight cardboard: one piece, 6 inches by 8 inches
Stiff notepaper: one piece, 8 inches by 8 inches; one piece, 4 inches by 4 inches; and six pieces, 4 inches by 6 inches
Cardboard tube: 1 inch in diameter and 5 inches long

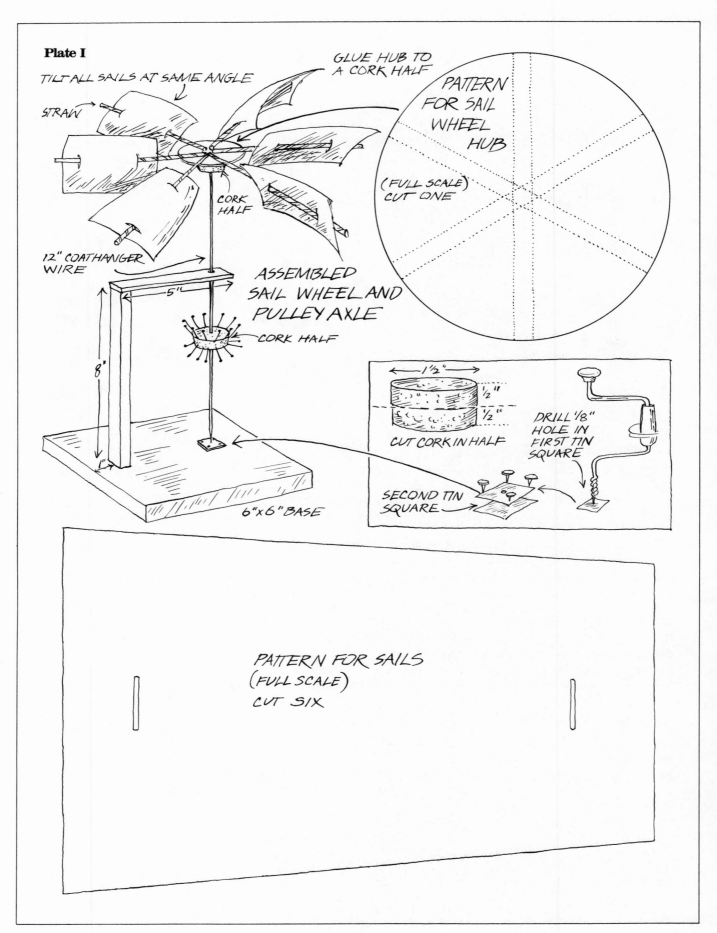

Plate I

TILT ALL SAILS AT SAME ANGLE

STRAW

GLUE HUB TO A CORK HALF

PATTERN FOR SAIL WHEEL HUB

(FULL SCALE) CUT ONE

CORK HALF

12" COATHANGER WIRE

ASSEMBLED SAIL WHEEL AND PULLEY AXLE

CORK HALF

5"

8"

4"

6"x6" BASE

1½"

½"

½"

CUT CORK IN HALF

SECOND TIN SQUARE

DRILL ⅛" HOLE IN FIRST TIN SQUARE

PATTERN FOR SAILS
(FULL SCALE)
CUT SIX

Tin: two pieces, 1 inch by 1 inch, from a can

Wire: one piece of 18-gauge, 6 inches long, and coat-hanger wire

Paint: enamel

To Build a Sunshine Engine

To make the base for the sail wheel (Plate I), nail the 8-inch length of 1/2-inch by 1/2-inch wood as an upright to the 6-inch square base by putting a nail in up through the bottom. It should be centered and 1 inch from the edge of the base as shown in the drawing. Drill a hole, 1/8 inch in diameter, in the 3/4- by 1/4- by 5-inch piece of wood, 1 inch from the end. This is the support arm. Nail the other end to the top of the upright.

To make the sail wheel and pulley axle (Plate I), cut a 12-inch length of coat-hanger wire. File one end to a point. Cut a 1 1/2-inch diameter cork into two 1/2-inch slices. Make a pulley by sticking pins in at an angle around both edges of one of the slices. Drop the wire axle through the hole in the support arm and push it through the cork pulley. The pulley should be centered about halfway between the support arm and the base. Drill a 1/8-inch hole in the center of one of the tin squares, and place this on top of the second tin square. Position the squares under the pointed end of the axle so that the axle rests in the hole, is perfectly vertical, and spins freely. Tack the squares into place.

To make sails (Plate I), cut the sail wheel hub of lightweight cardboard, following the pattern. Mark the center point on both sides of the second slice of cork. Glue the cardboard hub to one side of the cork, and push the other side onto the top of the axle wire, making sure that it is exactly centered and level. Glue six straws to the hub along the spoke lines, and cut six sails of stiff notepaper, following the pattern. Cut the slits in the sails and slip them onto the straws angling them all in the same direction. Test the wheel by blowing on it very gently. It should spin with the slightest breath of wind.

To make the engine base (Plate J), drill three 1/4-inch holes in the 6- by 10-inch piece of plywood, spaced as shown in the plan, to hold the three upright dowels. The two 10-inch dowels that support the flanged driving wheel and the flywheel must have 1/16-inch holes drilled through them. Do this 5 1/2 inches from the bottom and glue them into the two

parallel holes in the base. Take care that the holes are exactly in line. The 14-inch dowel is glued into the third hole in the base.

Cut the flanged driving wheel (Plates J and K) and the flywheel from stiff notepaper and the four washers from lightweight cardboard. Decorate the flywheel on both sides. Glue two straws to the flywheel for braces, as shown. Notch the straws where they cross so they lie flat. These will keep the flywheel from buckling.

Bend a 6-inch piece of 18-gauge wire to the shape shown for the engine axle. Push the long, straight end of the axle first through the center of the flywheel, then through the hole in the first dowel. Add the flanged driving wheel and push the axle through the hole in the second dowel. Center the driving wheel between the two uprights, leaving a space of 3/4 of an inch between the dowel and the flywheel. Make sure that both wheels are at right angles to the axle, and put a drop of glue on both sides of each to ensure that wheel and axle move together.

To make the walking beam (Plate J), you will need three drinking straws. Pierce three pinholes in a straw, 8 1/4 inches long, one in the exact center and one 1/2 inch in from each end. Fasten this straw to the 14-inch dowel, 9 inches up from the base, with a straight pin through the center hole. Cut another straw 6 inches long and make pinholes 1 inch from either end. Insert one end onto the end of the engine axle and pin the other end to the crossbeam straw. Bend the end of the pin so that it will not slip off.

Make a hole 1 inch from the end of the third 8 1/4-inch straw, and fasten it to the other end of the crossbeam with a bent pin. This forms the piston. Position a cardboard tube onto the base so that the piston drops into its exact center. Glue the tube in place. You can paint the tube and wooden parts all one color or a wonderful variety of colors.

To make a driving belt (Plate K), tie a long loop of thread around the flanged driving wheel and around the pulley on the sail wheel. Place the bases in a sunny window. The engine works best if the temperature of the room is fairly cool. Arrange the bases so that the driving belt is just taut. As the sun hits the surface of the floor or table under the engine, it warms the air, which rises and makes the sails turn. A floor or baseboard heat outlet will supply an equally effective column of rising air.

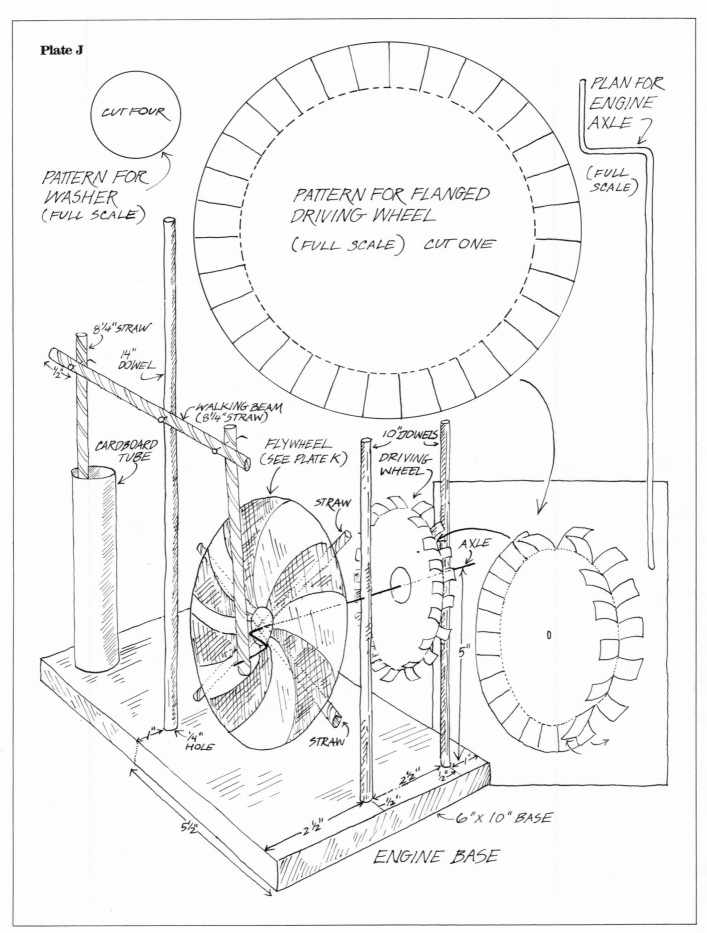

Plate J

CUT FOUR

PATTERN FOR WASHER (FULL SCALE)

PATTERN FOR FLANGED DRIVING WHEEL

(FULL SCALE) CUT ONE

PLAN FOR ENGINE AXLE

(FULL SCALE)

8¼" STRAW

14" DOWEL

½"

WALKING BEAM (8¼" STRAW)

CARDBOARD TUBE

FLYWHEEL (SEE PLATE K)

STRAW

10" DOWELS

DRIVING WHEEL

AXLE

STRAW

1"

¼" HOLE

STRAW

5"

1"

½"

2½"

½"

2½"

6" x 10" BASE

5½"

ENGINE BASE

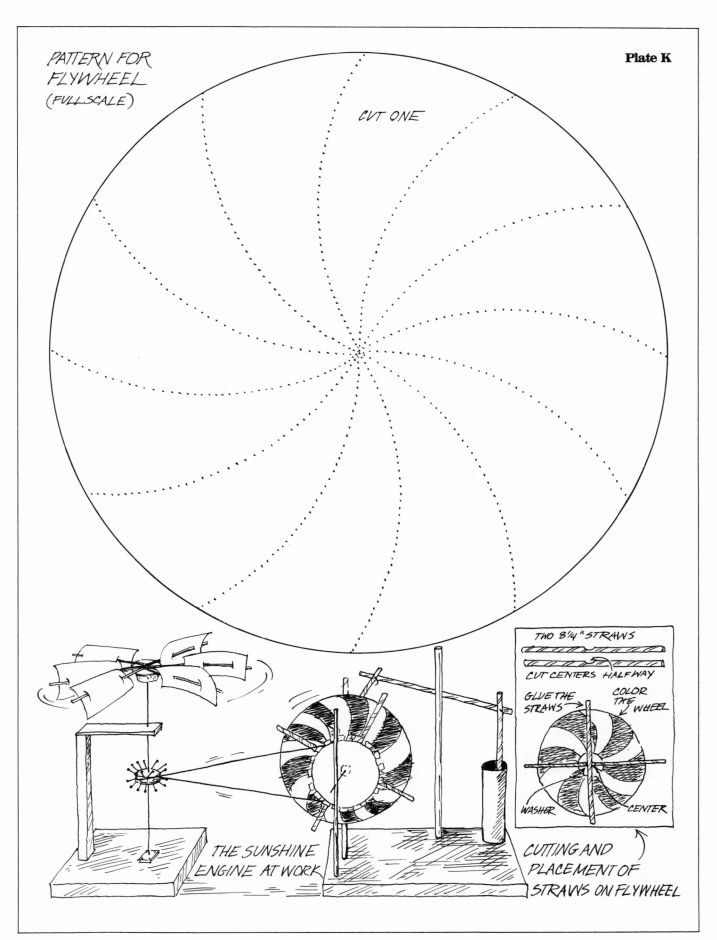

PATTERN FOR
FLYWHEEL
(FULLSCALE)

Plate K

CUT ONE

TWO 8¼" STRAWS

CUT CENTERS HALFWAY

GLUE THE
STRAWS

COLOR
THE
WHEEL

WASHER

CENTER

THE SUNSHINE
ENGINE AT WORK

CUTTING AND
PLACEMENT OF
STRAWS ON FLYWHEEL

A Short Treatise on Soldering

A number of projects in the book call for soldering. In some cases it is the only possible way to build the toy. In others it is not essential, but simply the neatest or most convenient way to produce a part. If you have never worked with a soldering iron, prepare for a new adventure. It may seem at first glance like a dangerous or exotic tool, but with a few precautions, there is no reason why children as well as adults should not become quite proficient in its use.

A 75-watt soldering iron is quite good enough for most jobs. You will need an iron rest, a roll of solid wire solder — 50 percent lead and 50 percent tin — and a small can of soldering paste. You will also need a brush to apply the paste and a moist cellulose sponge to clean the tip of the iron as you work.

Set up your work area with good light and ventilation and also a nonflammable surface where you can rest the iron when it is hot.

Practice with scraps of tin from a can until you feel confident using the iron. First heat the iron until it melts the solder on contact. Use the flat side of the iron, not the tip. Form a right angle from two pieces of scrap tin. Hold them together using masking tape on the outside of the angle. Now brush the inside of the angle with a 1/4-inch line of solder on both pieces. Melt a blob of solder onto the tin. Spread it with the iron all along the joint in a smooth, thin film. Add more solder, if necessary, until the entire joint is coated. Allow it to cool for a minute, remove the tape, and test the joint. Practice until you can make a strong clean joint with a minimum amount of solder. Keep the tip of your iron clean by wiping it frequently on the moist sponge.

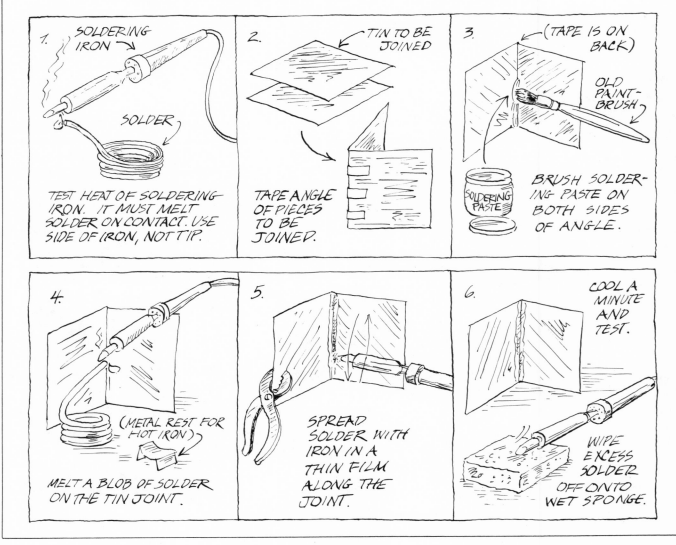

1. SOLDERING IRON
SOLDER
TEST HEAT OF SOLDERING IRON. IT MUST MELT SOLDER ON CONTACT. USE SIDE OF IRON, NOT TIP.

2. TIN TO BE JOINED
TAPE ANGLE OF PIECES TO BE JOINED.

3. (TAPE IS ON BACK)
OLD PAINT-BRUSH
SOLDERING PASTE
BRUSH SOLDERING PASTE ON BOTH SIDES OF ANGLE.

4. (METAL REST FOR HOT IRON)
MELT A BLOB OF SOLDER ON THE TIN JOINT.

5. SPREAD SOLDER WITH IRON IN A THIN FILM ALONG THE JOINT.

6. COOL A MINUTE AND TEST.
WIPE EXCESS SOLDER OFF ONTO WET SPONGE.

TIN STEAMBOAT

A jaunty toy steamboat — which doesn't actually run by steam, so in all honesty shouldn't be called one — may be made from directions that appeared in a children's paper in 1896. The mechanism is extremely simple, the propulsion being provided by a coil of copper or brass tubing that, when heated in the proper place, sets a current of water flowing through the tube with enough force to push the boat ahead. While the design of this boat could not be considered exactly streamlined, it does have a most endearing "African Queen" rakishness.

Tools and Materials

Soldering iron: 75-watt or stronger
Solder: solid wire, 50 percent lead and 50 percent tin
Soldering paste
Hammer
Pliers: needle-nose and bullnose
Paintbrush: small
Tin snips: small, duckbilled type are the easiest to use
Drill: with a 3/4-inch bit
Marks-on-anything pencil
Tracing paper: for patterns
Tin or galvanized metal sheeting: one piece, 12 inches by 12 inches, lightweight enough to be cut easily with tin snips. Get it from a sheet metal works.
Copper or brass tubing: 1/8-inch diameter, two or three 12-inch lengths to allow for practicing, available at many hobby shops
Wire: 14- and 18-gauge
Nails: one, small and one, 1/8-inch diameter
Emery cloth: medium grit
Masking tape
Lead: U-shaped came, available at stained-glass suppliers (if you cannot find came, use tire-balancing weights).
Paint: black, heat-resistant stove paint and marine or exterior enamel

To Build a Steamboat

To build the hull (Plates L and M), make patterns from the outlines given for the hull, keel, bottom, deckhouse, smokestack, rudder and rudder holder. Lay them on the sheet metal and trace around them carefully with a marks-on-anything pencil. Cut them along the solid lines. The broken lines indicate where they are to be bent; the dotted lines indicate where one piece of metal is to overlap another.

Drill a hole for the smokestack in the deckhouse with a drill and a 3/4-inch bit. Make slots on each side by hammering a small nail into the metal along the lines, making the holes as close together as possible. Turn the piece over and hammer the nail into the spaces between the holes until the slots are open the full length. Make the two small holes in the bottom of the boat with a 1/8-inch diameter nail. Smooth all of the edges with emery cloth.

Bend the two sides of the hull to conform to the curve of the bottom. Tape all three pieces together on the outside. Bend a 1 1/8-inch length of 18-gauge wire to the shape of the pintle and insert it in the stern of the boat, as shown. Tape it in place. Solder all of the joints on the inside of the hull, taking special care around the area of the pintle. If you have never used a soldering iron before, see the instructions in our Short Treatise on Soldering which appears on the previous page.

The next step is really the most difficult part of the whole business, that is bending the tubing coil (Plate N). You may spoil some before you get the hang of it. The trick is to hold the tubing with the bullnose pliers at the point where you want to start the bend and very gently bend the tube with your hand, just the smallest bit. Then move the pliers up to the bent part and bend again a little farther on, very gently. Slowly work the tube into the shape of the coil, as shown in the plan. If you try to bend the tubing too fast, it will crease or crack. Insert the ends of the coil through the holes in the bottom of the boat and solder them in place. You will find that the tubing will not accept the solder as readily as tin unless it is well heated first with the iron. Now test your boat for leaks by floating it in a basin of water. Resolder it where necessary.

Cut a length of 14-gauge wire 26 inches long and bend it in half, making a small loop where it bends (Plate N). Center the loop on the stern, as shown in the helm plan, and shape the wire to fit the edge of the hull on both sides. Hold it in place with masking tape every few inches. Solder it to the hull along the bottom

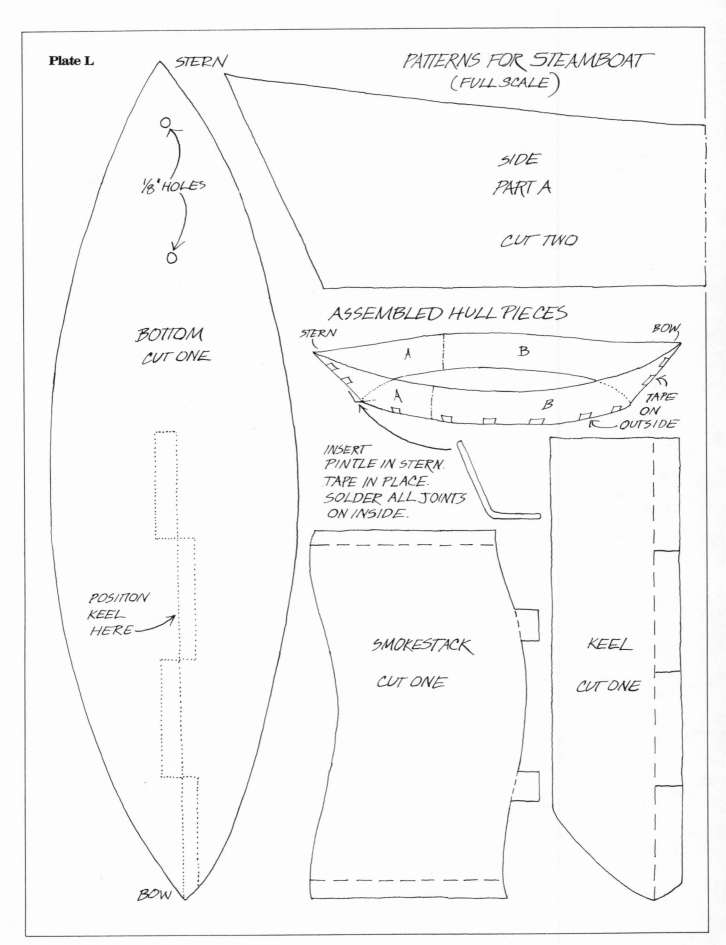

Plate L

STERN

PATTERNS FOR STEAMBOAT
(FULL SCALE)

1/8" HOLES

SIDE
PART A

CUT TWO

BOTTOM
CUT ONE

ASSEMBLED HULL PIECES

STERN   BOW

A   B

A   B   TAPE
ON
OUTSIDE

INSERT
PINTLE IN STERN.
TAPE IN PLACE.
SOLDER ALL JOINTS
ON INSIDE.

POSITION
KEEL
HERE

SMOKESTACK

CUT ONE

KEEL

CUT ONE

BOW

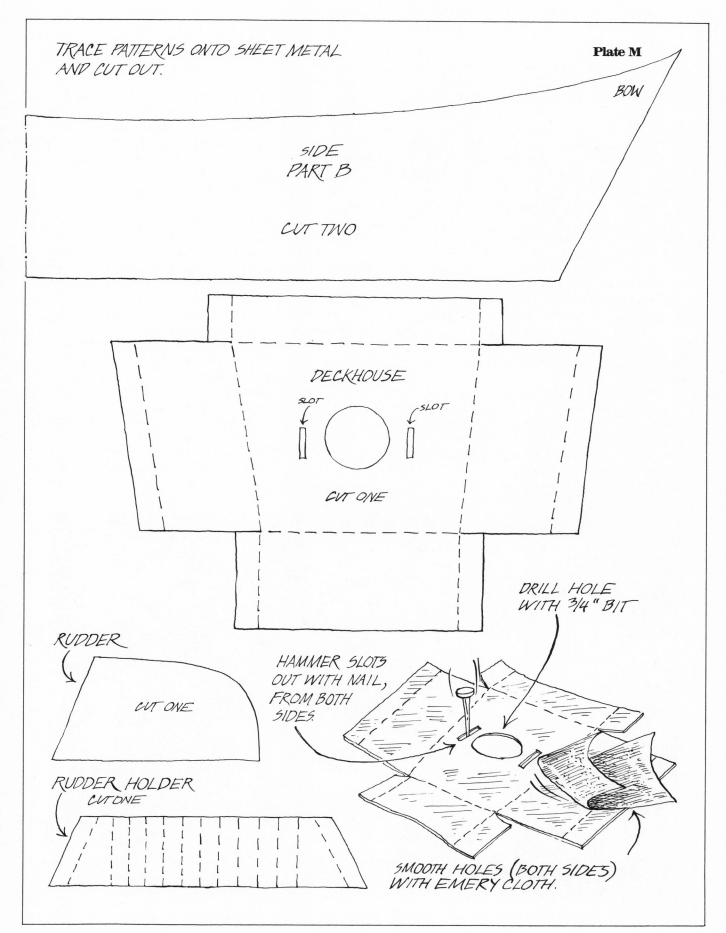

TRACE PATTERNS ONTO SHEET METAL
AND CUT OUT.

BOW

SIDE
PART B

CUT TWO

DECKHOUSE

SLOT   SLOT

CUT ONE

DRILL HOLE
WITH 3/4" BIT

RUDDER

CUT ONE

HAMMER SLOTS
OUT WITH NAIL,
FROM BOTH
SIDES.

RUDDER HOLDER
CUT ONE

SMOOTH HOLES (BOTH SIDES)
WITH EMERY CLOTH.

side of the wire. This not only strengthens the hull, but it also provides a finish for the gunwale and a loop to hold the rudder head.

To make the tiller and rudder (Plates N and O), bend a length of 18-gauge wire to the shape shown for the tiller in the plans and solder the rudder to it. Bend the rudder holder in the corrugated fashion along the broken lines and solder it in place. This will hold the tiller in any position in which it is set.

Bend the flaps of the keel down at right angles to the keel itself (Plate O), to the right and left. Solder it to the bottom of the boat, where indicated on the pattern. The keel will need to be weighted along the bottom edge so that the boat will not capsize. Use lead came if you can find some or tire balancing weights if you cannot. Solder the lead to the keel, taking care not to let the iron touch the lead for more than a second, as it will melt very quickly if overheated. Add lead until the boat rides nicely level.

Assemble the deckhouse (Plate O) by bending the metal to right angles along the broken lines. You can make a nice sharp angle by holding the piece to be bent along the edge of the work surface and gently tapping down along the fold line with a hammer. Solder the corners.

To make the smokestack, bend the metal along the broken lines the length of the stack; then roll the piece around a broomstick to form a tube, engaging the folds as shown in the plans. Pinch the folds tightly together with needle-nose pliers. Insert the tabs on the smokestack into the slits on the deckhouse roof and bend them outward. Fit the deckhouse into the hull as far as the dotted lines so that it just covers the coil, and solder it into place.

Clean the boat well with paint thinner or soap and water to remove any excess soldering paste. Give the hull a coat of metal primer. Then paint it with enamel. Paint the deckhouse and smokestack with heat resistant black paint.

To operate the boat you must provide a heat source. A small, homemade alcohol burner is the most efficient source of heat for this purpose, as it can be built so that it directs the flame to a precise spot. This is important in the case of your steamboat; its operation depends on the coil being heated at exactly the right place. You will have to experiment to find this spot, but it is somewhere on the curve where the lower tube curls up into the coil. Directions for building the alcohol burner are on page 41.

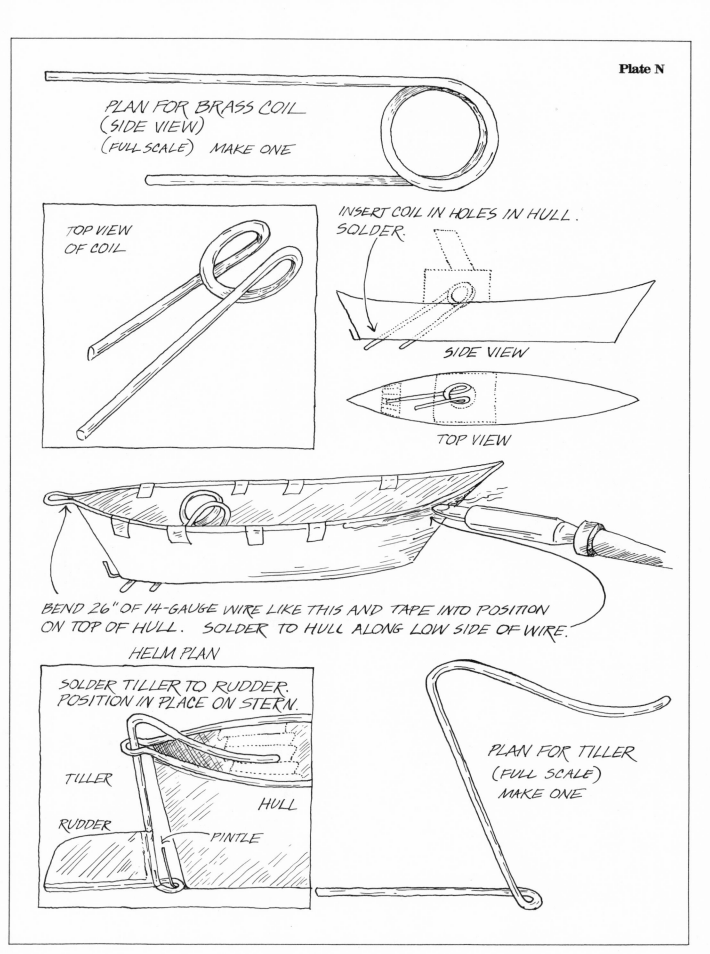

Plate N

PLAN FOR BRASS COIL
(SIDE VIEW)
(FULL SCALE) MAKE ONE

TOP VIEW
OF COIL

INSERT COIL IN HOLES IN HULL.
SOLDER.

SIDE VIEW

TOP VIEW

BEND 26" OF 14-GAUGE WIRE LIKE THIS AND TAPE INTO POSITION
ON TOP OF HULL. SOLDER TO HULL ALONG LOW SIDE OF WIRE.

HELM PLAN

SOLDER TILLER TO RUDDER.
POSITION IN PLACE ON STERN.

TILLER

HULL

RUDDER

PINTLE

PLAN FOR TILLER
(FULL SCALE)
MAKE ONE

Plate O

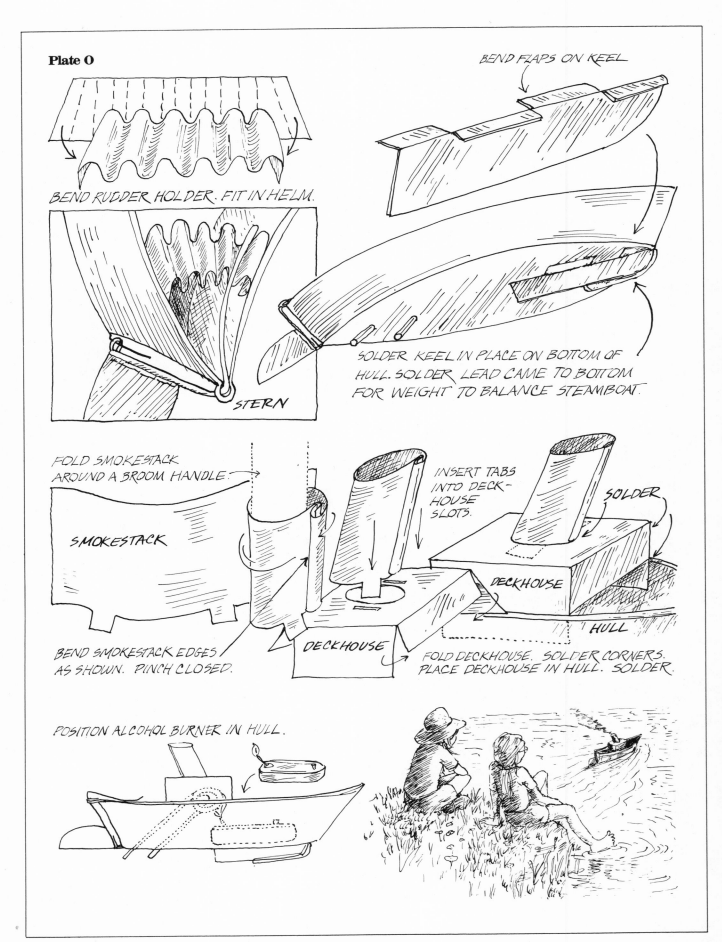

BEND RUDDER HOLDER. FIT IN HELM.

BEND FLAPS ON KEEL

SOLDER KEEL IN PLACE ON BOTTOM OF HULL. SOLDER LEAD CAME TO BOTTOM FOR WEIGHT TO BALANCE STEAMBOAT.

STERN

FOLD SMOKESTACK AROUND A BROOM HANDLE.

SMOKESTACK

INSERT TABS INTO DECK-HOUSE SLOTS.

SOLDER

DECKHOUSE

HULL

DECKHOUSE

BEND SMOKESTACK EDGES AS SHOWN. PINCH CLOSED.

FOLD DECKHOUSE. SOLDER CORNERS. PLACE DECKHOUSE IN HULL. SOLDER.

POSITION ALCOHOL BURNER IN HULL.

HERON'S STEAM ENGINE

Two hundred years ago a Scottish boy named Jamie Watt became so fascinated while watching his mother's teakettle that he went right out and invented the steam engine. This is one version of an old schoolbook story, and for years children believed this was really the way it happened. It was true in a way; James Watt did do major work to perfect the steam engines that in turn powered our industrial revolution. But the use of steam power has a much longer history.

Almost 2,000 years ago, a very clever Greek inventor, Heron of Alexandria, devised the "Aeolipile," a type of steam turbine. The "Aeolipile" was a metal sphere with a curved jet on each side. Steam was forced through these jets and caused the sphere to whirl. There is no record that any practical use was made of Heron's invention. It was only something to watch with amazement. Our model is even more primitive than Heron's, but with a little imagination, it can be put to some useful work.

Tools and Materials

Alcohol lamp (see pages 39 and 40)
Tin snips
Hacksaw
Metal file
Wire cutters
Hammer
Drill: with a 5/16-inch bit and a 1/8-inch bit
Paintbrush: small
Soldering iron
Solder
Soldering paste
Brass tubing: 1/8-inch diameter — two pieces, 3/4 inch long
Nails: 3/4 inch long and a large blunt one
Carpet tacks
Small tin can
Paint: enamel
Wire coat hanger
Wood: one piece, 6 inches by 6 inches by 1/2 inch; two pieces, 1 inch by 3/8 inch by 9 inches; one piece, 1 inch by 3/8 inch by 6 3/4 inches
Tin: one piece 1 inch by 7 inches cut from a heavy can and well flattened
Cork: one small to plug a 3/8-inch hole

To Build a Steam Engine

To make the boiler, first drill a hole 5/16 inch in diameter in the top of an unopened 6-ounce can of some liquid and empty it. This hole should be 1/4 inch from the rim of the can. Make a 1/8-inch hole in the exact center of the can lid. Make two more 1/8-inch holes in the sides of the can, 1/4 inch below the top rim and exactly opposite each other. Make a 1/8-inch hole in the exact center of the can bottom.

Cut an 8-inch length of straight coat-hanger wire. Sand it well to remove any finish and file one end to a point. Push the pointed end of the wire through the hole in the top of the can and out the hole in the bottom until 1 inch of the pointed end shows. Solder the wire in the places where the can and wire meet so the seals are watertight.

To make the steam jets, close off one end of each of two 3/4-inch lengths of brass tubing by melting a dab of solder over the ends. Make a small hole 1/4 inch from the closed end of each tube by sawing partway through the tubing

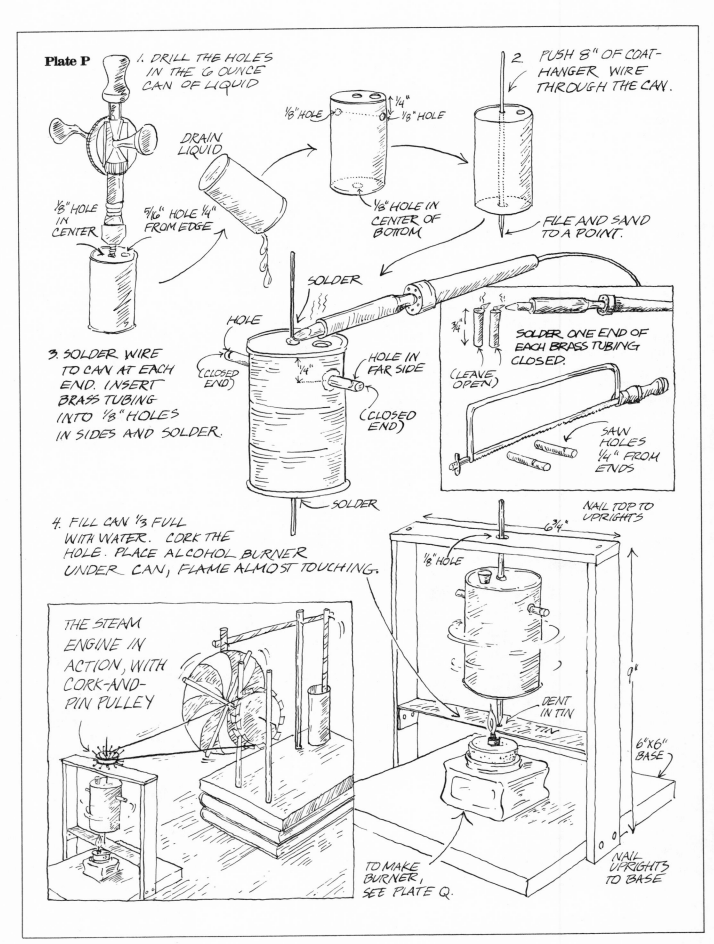

Plate P

1. DRILL THE HOLES IN THE 6 OUNCE CAN OF LIQUID

1/8" HOLE — 1/8" HOLE — 1/4"

DRAIN LIQUID

1/8" HOLE IN CENTER

5/16" HOLE 1/4" FROM EDGE

1/8" HOLE IN CENTER OF BOTTOM

2. PUSH 8" OF COAT-HANGER WIRE THROUGH THE CAN.

FILE AND SAND TO A POINT.

SOLDER

HOLE

(CLOSED END)

1/4"

HOLE IN FAR SIDE

(CLOSED END)

3. SOLDER WIRE TO CAN AT EACH END. INSERT BRASS TUBING INTO 1/8" HOLES IN SIDES AND SOLDER.

3/4"

(LEAVE OPEN)

SOLDER ONE END OF EACH BRASS TUBING CLOSED.

SAW HOLES 1/4" FROM ENDS

SOLDER

4. FILL CAN 1/3 FULL WITH WATER. CORK THE HOLE. PLACE ALCOHOL BURNER UNDER CAN, FLAME ALMOST TOUCHING.

THE STEAM ENGINE IN ACTION, WITH CORK-AND-PIN PULLEY

NAIL TOP TO UPRIGHTS

6 3/4"

1/8" HOLE

9"

DENT IN TIN

TIN

6"x6" BASE

NAIL UPRIGHTS TO BASE

TO MAKE BURNER, SEE PLATE Q.

with a hacksaw. Make sure that the insides of the tubes are not blocked with solder between the holes and the open end by running water through them. Solder the open ends of the tubes into the holes in the sides of the can. The tubes should be at right angles to the can, the holes facing to the side (not up or down) and going in the same direction. Fill the can with water through the top hole and test it to make sure that the steam jets are not clogged with solder by pouring the water out through them. If it is okay, cork it.

To make the base, nail the 9-inch uprights to the 6- by 6-inch base, as shown in the diagram. Make a slight dent in the exact center of the 1- by 7-inch strip of tin with a hammer and large, blunt nail. This makes the pivot point for the boiler axle. Bend down 1/2 inch of each end of the strip and tack it to the uprights, 2 1/2 inches above the base. Drill a 1/8-inch hole in the exact center of the 6 3/4-inch crosspiece. Insert the top of the wire boiler axle through

the hole, set the pointed end of the axle in the dent in the tin support, and nail the crosspiece to the uprights. The boiler should turn freely and the axle should be exactly vertical when all is assembled. You can paint all the wooden parts.

Now fill your boiler about one-third full of water. If the water is already boiling, you won't have to wait for it. Set an alcohol lamp under one side of the boiler with the flame not quite touching the bottom of the boiler. (See below.) When the water again reaches a boil, the steam will be forced out of the jets, and the boiler will begin to revolve — slowly at first, then faster and faster.

If you want to put your engine to work, make a cork and pin pulley such as used in the Sunshine Engine. Put the pulley on the boiler axle above the crosspiece. Connect it to the flanged wheel on the sunshine engine. You can invent your own contraptions to be powered by this steam engine too.

Making Alcohol Burners for Toys

There are several steam projects that call for a small size heat source. The easiest thing to use is a candle, but candles have an unpleasant way of depositing soot on boilers, fingers, and noses. Small cans of sterno are also possible, but they heat too wide an area and can be expensive if you use many. The burner from a chafing dish or fondue pot will work, if it will fit into the available space. The neatest solution, however, is to custom design the burner best suited to your project.

Whatever heater you use, be careful with it. Be sure that it is firmly based so that it will not tip or be knocked over. Never leave lighted burners unattended. Younger children should be supervised at all times when using them.

BURNER FOR HERON'S STEAM ENGINE

Tools and Materials

Razor knife
Hacksaw
Hammer

Glass bottle: a short, squat one with a wide mouth, 1 1/2 inches to 2 inches high by 1 1/2 to 2 inches square. Vitamin pills and inks are often packaged in such bottles.
Cork: to fit the bottle
Candle wick: about 8 inches long, the kind without wire in the middle
Brass tubing: 5/32-inch diameter, or just large enough for the wick, about 2 inches long or 1/2 inch longer than the cork.
Nail: 1/8-inch diameter
Alcohol lamp fuel (denatured alcohol)

To Make Steam Engine Burner

Make a hole through the center of the cork with a 1/8-inch diameter nail and push the tubing through this hole. There should be about 1/4 inch of tubing showing at both the top and bottom. Thread the wick through the tubing until about 1/4 inch shows at the top. Cut a shallow groove up one side of the cork to let air into the bottle. Pour lamp fuel into the bottle,

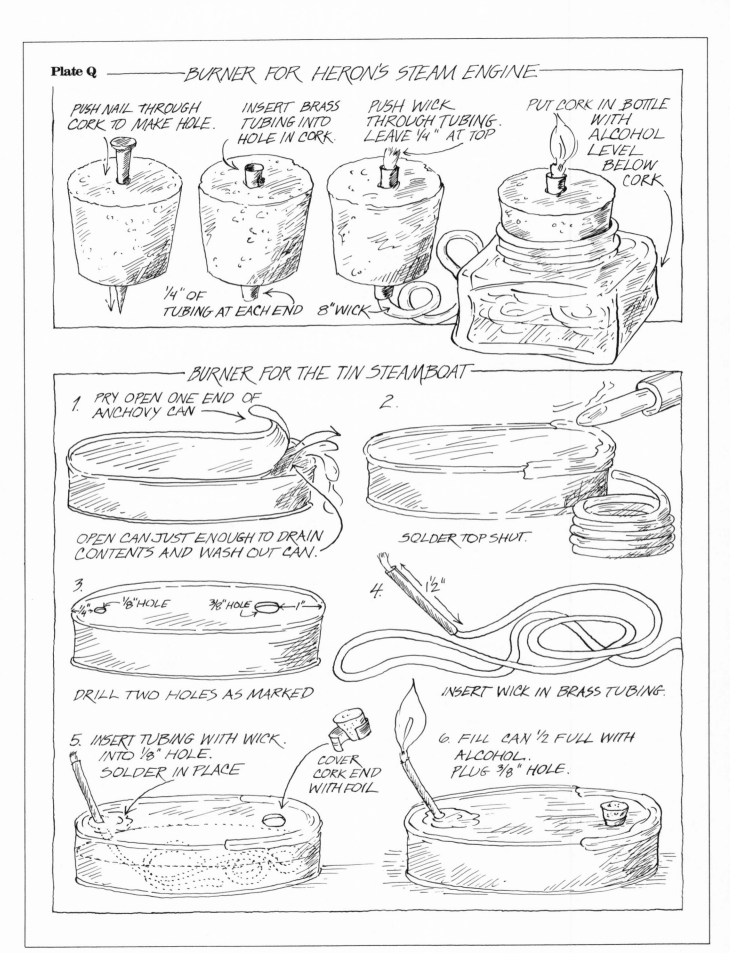

Plate Q ———— BURNER FOR HERON'S STEAM ENGINE————

PUSH NAIL THROUGH CORK TO MAKE HOLE.

INSERT BRASS TUBING INTO HOLE IN CORK.

PUSH WICK THROUGH TUBING. LEAVE 1/4" AT TOP

PUT CORK IN BOTTLE WITH ALCOHOL LEVEL BELOW CORK

1/4" OF TUBING AT EACH END

8" WICK

——— BURNER FOR THE TIN STEAMBOAT———

1. PRY OPEN ONE END OF ANCHOVY CAN

OPEN CAN JUST ENOUGH TO DRAIN CONTENTS AND WASH OUT CAN.

2. SOLDER TOP SHUT.

3. 1/4" 1/8" HOLE 3/8" HOLE 1"

DRILL TWO HOLES AS MARKED

4. 1/2"

INSERT WICK IN BRASS TUBING.

5. INSERT TUBING WITH WICK INTO 1/8" HOLE. SOLDER IN PLACE

COVER CORK END WITH FOIL

6. FILL CAN 1/2 FULL WITH ALCOHOL. PLUG 3/8" HOLE.

but keep the level well below the cork so that it will not absorb any fuel. Let the burner stand until the wick is saturated, then light it, and fire up the boiler.

BURNER FOR THE TIN STEAMBOAT

Tools and Materials

Soldering iron
Solder: solid wire, 50 percent lead and 50 percent tin
Soldering paste
Pliers
Hacksaw
Hammer
Drill: with a 3/8-inch bit
Anchovy can: a long oval, approximately 1 1/2 inches by 4 inches. Make sure it is not aluminum — look for one with a rim on both the top and the bottom.
Cork: to fit a 3/8-inch hole
Brass tubing: 1/8-inch diameter and 1 1/2 inches long
Nail: 1/8-inch diameter
Candle wick: 8 inches long, the kind without wire in the middle
Aluminum foil
Alcohol lamp fuel (denatured alcohol)

To Make the Steamboat Burner

Open the anchovy can just far enough to extract the contents. Don't roll it up on the key as you normally would; only start it and then open it up the rest of the way with pliers so that you bend as little of the lid as possible. Wash it out thoroughly, unless of course you want your boat to smell like a fishing trawler. Bend the lid back into place and solder it closed. Drill a 3/8-inch hole, 1 inch from one end and make a 1/8-inch hole at the other end about 1/4 inch from the rim. You can make the 1/8-inch hole with a nail.

Cut a 1 1/2-inch length of tubing and insert the wick through the tubing. Make it a good, long piece of wick, as it will be nearly impossible to replace once the burner is assembled. Push all of the long end of the wick through the 1/8-inch hole in the can, and insert the tubing into the can about 1/4 inch or less. Solder the tubing into place with a great deal of care so that there is no possibility of leakage around the base of the tube. Fill the can about halfway with alcohol. Wrap the cork with aluminum foil so it will not absorb any fuel and plug the hole. Bend the tube gently outward until the wick is just below the steamboat coil, as described in the Tin Steamboat directions.

PART TWO

GRAVITY POWERED TOYS

Nothing to Do but Weight

Gravity is one of the most versatile and easily harnessed forces used to make toys move. It motivates a wide range of mechanisms from the most basic of rocking toys to the intricate sand wheel pictures. From the eighteenth century on, the most widespread and popular toy using gravity was the rocking horse. Many were elaborately carved and painted. Some had tails and manes made from real horsehair.

The nineteenth century produced a great interest in science, and the how-to books for children went into great detail about what made things work. One of the favorite topics was gravity — methods for finding the center of gravity by experimentation and the making of toys to illustrate this principle.

The Seesaw and Galloping Horse toys in this book are based on the pendulum and are quite easy to build. The Seesaw can be cut out and put together in a couple of hours. Painting will take longer, of course, depending on how detailed a job you wish to make of it. If the figures are carved from wood, you will probably want to take a good deal of time to make them attractive and lifelike. The mechanism for the Galloping Horse can be put together very quickly. Then it is up to you how many horses, riders, and backgrounds you want to draw and color.

We found the original for this toy in the Museum of Childhood in Edinburgh, Scotland, along with another of a similar nature — a theater box with several occupants, each nodding its head to a different pendulum swing. This museum is a very special place and well worth a visit. It was started in 1955 by Patrick Murray, a city councilor and convener of the Edinburgh Museums Committee. What began as a modest exhibit occupying part of an existing city museum grew to a sizable collection housed in its own four-story building in Hyndford's Close. Mr. Murray himself was curator for many years, and his personality is still delightfully evident in the humorous and informal labels identifying the various objects.

Our third gravity project, the Leotard Sand Toy, is a much more sophisticated application of the principle and will take you six to eight hours to complete. The work involves precision, as it must be assembled accurately, but it is by no means difficult. These toys have an interesting history. Throughout the eighteenth century and earlier, there was great enthusiasm for intricate mechanical toys and automatons. Some of these creations were so marvelously lifelike and could perform such complicated tasks that their inventors were often suspected of witchcraft. Of course they were much too expensive to be owned by any but Eastern potentates and crowned heads. Some were carried about Europe and America to be shown at exhibitions. They created a strong desire for an inexpensive substitute that the average person could afford. In the mid-nineteenth century, the demand was finally met by the development of tin clockwork toys with simple windup mechanisms and the sand motor. Do-it-yourself sand toys, very similar to ours, were sold as printed sheets with instructions on how to cut them out and put them together.

These small figures mounted on half of a lead bullet were called Prussians in Paris. "They were formed into battalions and being made to fall down, by drawing a rod over them, immediately started up again as soon as it was removed. We think that the figure of a beau, or a master of ceremonies, is much more appropriate for this trick, than that of a soldier; as the latter seldom bows, while, by the former, the most profound inclinations are often performed."

This jolly sailor spins and tips on the point of the needle, but he never falls. He was a popular nineteenth-century toy, illustrating the principle that if the center of gravity of a body is below its point of support, it cannot be overturned.

Horses with and without riders, prancing and rearing perilously near the edges of tables, served to prove the same principle.

Wolfgang de Kempelin's chess-playing automaton was introduced to an awed public in 1769 on the heels of a series of marvelous clockwork figures that played flutes and wrote letters. It was considered the most wonderful of all as it seemingly could reason and win at chess against all comers. Of course it was a fake. The machinery was made of cardboard and the man who was concealed inside could see the moves on the board by means of an elaborate arrangement of magnets.

GALLOPING HORSE AND RIDERS

The prototype of this mid-nineteenth-century toy is in the Museum of Childhood in Edinburgh, Scotland. There are many variations on the pendulum toy, but this one with its interchangeable horses and riders is particularly interesting. There is no reason to stop with the patterns in the book. You could design a whole set of cavalry officers or knights on chargers or cowboys and Indians, each with a suitable background scene.

Tools and Materials

Saw
Scissors
Soldering iron
Drill: with 1/8-inch bit and countersink bit
Solder: 50 percent lead and 50 percent tin
Soldering paste
Wire coat hanger
Wood: three pieces, each 3 1/2 inches by 3/4 inch by 12 inches long
Plumb bob: 3 1/2 inches long
White glue
Cardboard: lightweight
Plastic tubing: 1/8-inch diameter — one piece, 3 inches long
Felt-tip pen: black
Colored pencils or oil pastels
Wood screws: four, 1 inch long
Wire: 18-gauge
Sandpaper

To Build the Galloping Horse and Riders

To make the base (Plate A), sand the three wood pieces. Mark the lengthwise center line on two of the pieces and drill a 1/8-inch hole in each, on the line and 3/4 of an inch from one end. Center these uprights, as shown, on either side of the third board, which forms the base. The 1/8-inch holes must be level and directly opposite each other. At the bottoms of these pieces drill holes, as shown, and countersink two screws through each upright into the base.

To make the pendulum (Plate A), cut a straight piece of coat-hanger wire 13 1/2 inches long. Sand it well to remove any paint and make a right-angle bend in it 6 inches from one end. Cut a 3-inch piece of 18-gauge wire, and bend it up 1/2 inch on either end. Solder this onto the long end of the coat-hanger

wire, as shown. Three inches above this point, solder on a 1-inch wire which has been bent into a fishhook shape.

Cut a 7 1/2-inch length of coat-hanger wire and sand it clean. Insert one end of this wire into the top of a plumb bob, and bend it or melt a blob of solder on the end of the wire to hold it in place.

Insert the short end of the bent wire through the holes in the upright. Put two 1 1/4-inch pieces of plastic tubing on the wire between the uprights to act as spacers. Melt a blob of solder onto the end of the wire outside the upright to hold it in place. Bend the end of the plumb bob wire around the axle wire between the two pieces of tubing and solder in place.

To make the horse and rider (Plates A and B), trace the patterns on light cardboard, color, and cut out. Glue cardboard loops to the reverse side of the horse and rider. Position the loops so that the rider hangs on the fishhook and the horse hangs on the wire crosspiece below. The boy's foot fits into the stirrup, but the lady should have an extra loop put on the back of her skirt to slip over the stirrup. Paint a backdrop scene for the rider and attach it to the pendulum base.

1/8" HOLE IN CENTER OF UPRIGHT

BACKGROUND AND FIGURES ARE HOOKED TO THE PENDULUM ARM (MADE FROM 13 1/2" COAT-HANGER WIRE.)

1" WIRE

3" PIECE OF 18-GAUGE WIRE

3"

PLAN FOR PENDULUM ARM (FULL SCALE)

Plate A

1/8" HOLE IN CENTER OF UPRIGHT
1 1/4" PLASTIC TUBING SPACER

7 1/2" COATHANGER WIRE, SANDED AND INSERTED INTO PLUMB BOB

3 1/2" PLUMB BOB

ASSEMBLED PENDULUM BASE

CUT ONE

CUT ONE

CUT ONE

CUT ONE

PATTERNS FOR RIDERS (FULL SCALE)

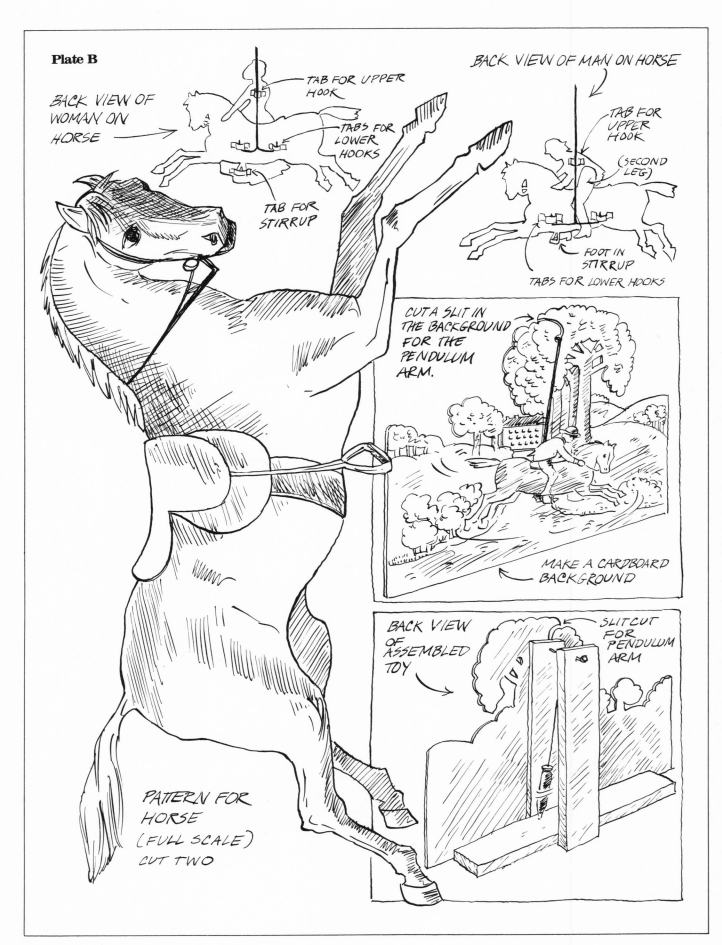

Plate B

BACK VIEW OF WOMAN ON HORSE →

TAB FOR UPPER HOOK

TABS FOR LOWER HOOKS

TAB FOR STIRRUP

BACK VIEW OF MAN ON HORSE

TAB FOR UPPER HOOK

(SECOND LEG)

FOOT IN STIRRUP

TABS FOR LOWER HOOKS

CUT A SLIT IN THE BACKGROUND FOR THE PENDULUM ARM.

MAKE A CARDBOARD BACKGROUND

BACK VIEW OF ASSEMBLED TOY →

SLIT CUT FOR PENDULUM ARM

PATTERN FOR HORSE (FULL SCALE) CUT TWO

SEESAW

This seesaw is a delightful toy for a child's bedside table, perfect for those dreamy moments just before sleep. A light tap sets the seesaw in motion, and the small figures go up and down, gaily swinging their arms and legs. This version has a boy and girl in Victorian costumes, but you could change them to bears or clowns instead. The figures may be cut from plywood and the details painted on or, if you enjoy whittling, carved in low relief from solid wood, as we did.

Tools and Materials

Coping saw
Needle-nose pliers
Knife: a sharp paring or jackknife
Drill: with a 1/8-inch bit and a 3/32-inch bit
Plywood: 1/2 inch — one piece, 6 inches by 12 inches or the same size in solid wood
Plywood: 1/4 inch — one piece, 3 inches by 12 inches or the same size in solid wood
Wood: one piece, 3/4 inch by 2 1/2 inches by 12 inches
Wire coat hanger
Wire: 22-gauge
Beads: fourteen, 1/4-inch diameter
Screw eyes: two 1/4-inch
Wood screws: four 1/2-inch
Fishing line or strong thread: 8 inches long
Fishing weight, one 6-oz. round weight
Sandpaper: fine
Paint: primer
Paint: model, artist's acrylic, or oil
White glue
Plastic tubing: 1/4-inch diameter, one inch long

To Build a Seesaw

To make the base (Plate D), sand the 3/4- by 2 1/2- by 12-inch base piece. Cut the seesaw and uprights from either 1/2-inch plywood or solid wood, following the pattern. Shape the ends and sand. Mark the exact center of the base piece. Draw a line down the center of each upright from top to bottom. Drill 1/8-inch holes on the uprights and seesaw, where shown on patterns. Drill a 3/32-inch hole in the underside of the seesaw for the pendulum shaft. Fix two screw eyes in the underside of the seesaw, 2 inches on either side of the center hole.

To make the pendulum (Plate D) cut a 2 3/4-inch piece of wire from the coat hanger. Bend one end through the loop in the fishing weight, squeeze — or solder — the bend tight so that the weight and wire are rigid. Apply glue to the other end of the wire and insert the wire in the hole at the underside of the seesaw; let it dry. Tie a length of fishing line or thread from each screw eye to the loop of the fishing weight, as shown. Screw the uprights to the base, making sure they are centered and that the axle holes line up. To make the figures (Plate C) cut, shape, and sand the pieces following the patterns. Use the coping saw for this. The torsos are cut from 1/2-inch wood. The arms, legs, thighs, and skirts are cut from 1/4-inch wood. The lower legs, thighs, and skirt pieces must be shaved down to 1/8 inch thick at the points where they overlap. These are indicated by dotted lines on the patterns. Remember that the arms, legs, and skirts must be cut in pairs. Drill 3/32-inch holes where shown at the knee and shoulder joints. Sand lightly; then paint with primer.

Let the primer dry; then paint in any colors desired. Glue the torsos, skirt sides, and thighs to the seesaw. Wire the arms to the torsos. Use light wire for this and insert a bead as a washer between each piece. Finish on either side with another bead and a wire loop. Fasten at the knees with a bead on either side and a single bead between the knees. The arms and legs should be loose enough to swing freely. Cut a 3 1/2-inch piece of coat-hanger wire for an axle. Run this through one upright, the seesaw, and the other upright. Use a 1/2-inch piece of plastic tubing on each side of the seesaw to keep it centered between the uprights. Finish the wire ends with small squares of wood or wooden beads. On our Seesaw, one figure was more vigorous than the other.

Plate C

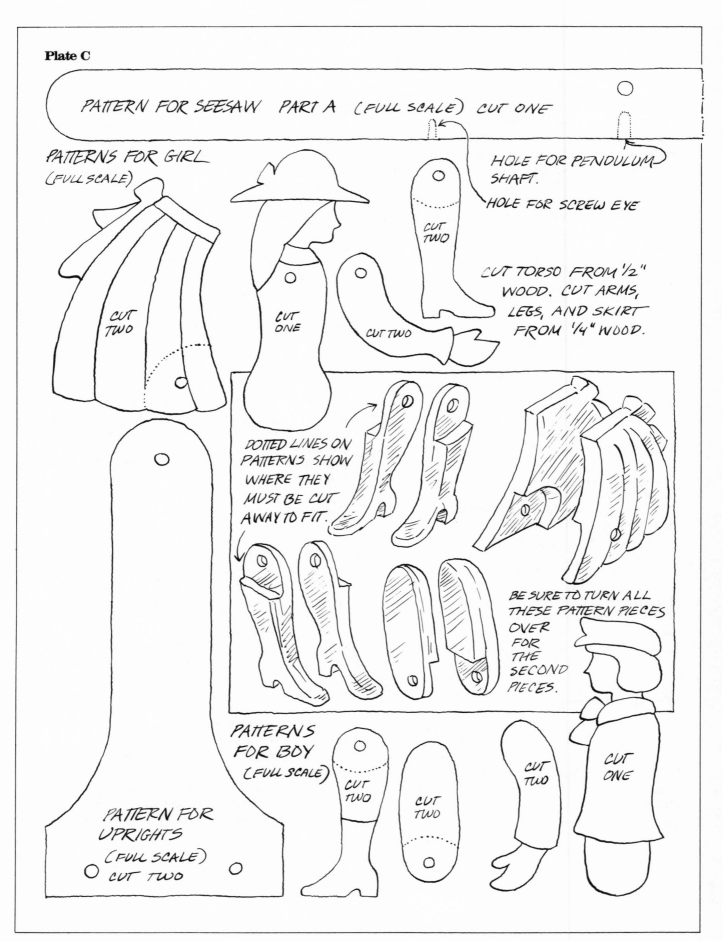

PATTERN FOR SEESAW   PART A   (FULL SCALE)   CUT ONE

PATTERNS FOR GIRL
(FULL SCALE)

HOLE FOR PENDULUM SHAFT.

HOLE FOR SCREW EYE

CUT TWO

CUT TWO

CUT ONE

CUT TWO

CUT TORSO FROM ½" WOOD. CUT ARMS, LEGS, AND SKIRT FROM ¼" WOOD.

DOTTED LINES ON PATTERNS SHOW WHERE THEY MUST BE CUT AWAY TO FIT.

BE SURE TO TURN ALL THESE PATTERN PIECES OVER FOR THE SECOND PIECES.

PATTERNS FOR BOY (FULL SCALE)

CUT TWO

CUT TWO

CUT TWO

CUT ONE

PATTERN FOR UPRIGHTS
(FULL SCALE)
CUT TWO

Plate D

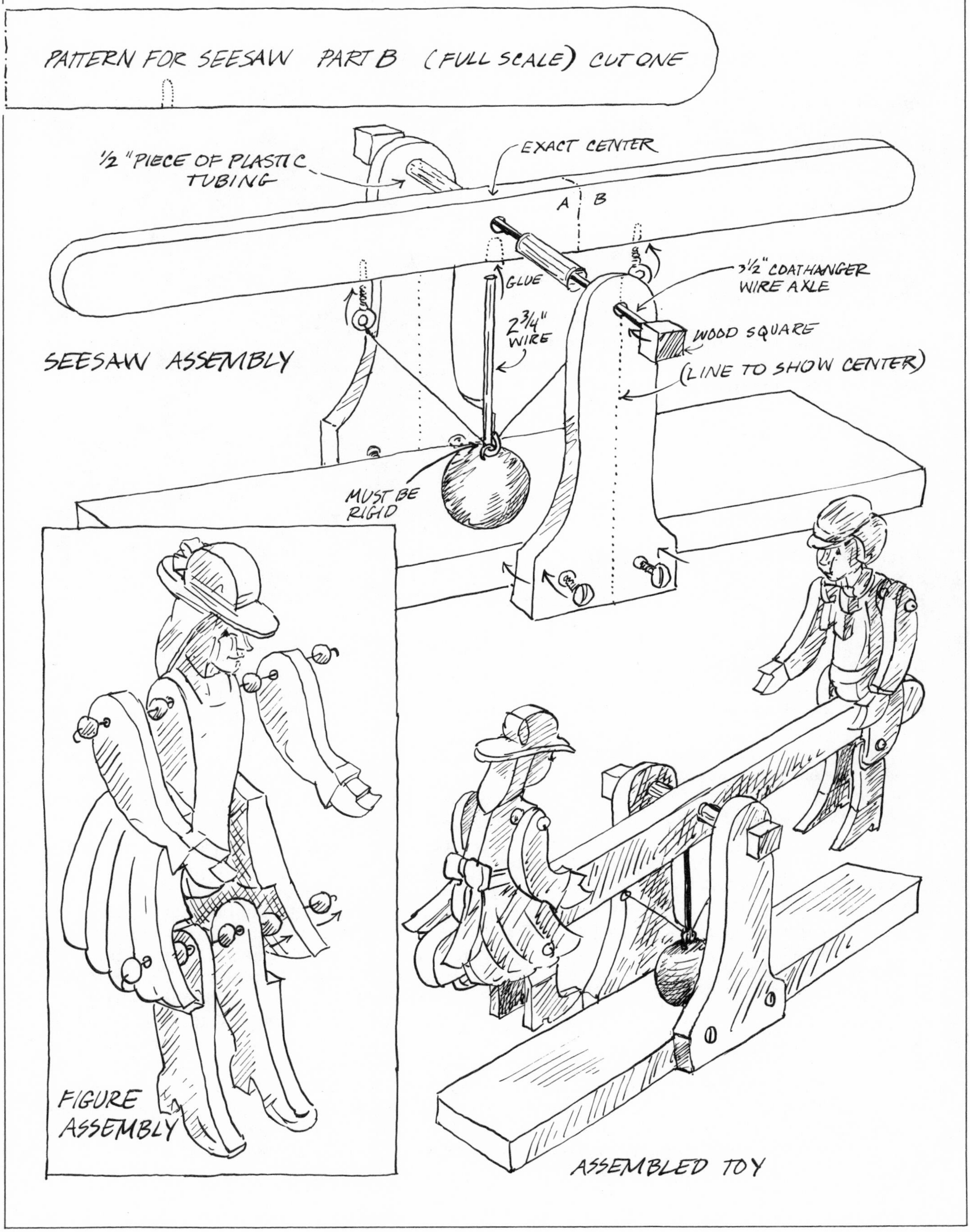
PATTERN FOR SEESAW PART B (FULL SCALE) CUT ONE
1/2" PIECE OF PLASTIC TUBING
EXACT CENTER
A
B
GLUE
3 1/2" COATHANGER WIRE AXLE
2 3/4" WIRE
WOOD SQUARE
SEESAW ASSEMBLY
(LINE TO SHOW CENTER)
MUST BE RIGID
FIGURE ASSEMBLY
ASSEMBLED TOY

LEOTARD SAND TOY

For over a hundred years, sand toys have intrigued and perplexed children and grownups alike. Kenneth Grahame, in his autobiography *Dream Days,* writes of the "wonderfully unsolved mystery" of a small acrobat silently tumbling in a glass-fronted box. He evokes the enchantment we all feel before these marvelously inventive creations. There are no keys to turn or batteries to replace, only the ritual turning of the box that sets a miniature world into motion. The Leotard — named after a famous French aerialist of the nineteenth century — was a popular subject for sand toys, but you could make many variations using the same mechanism but changing the acrobat's appearance.

Tools and Materials

Scissors
Razor knife
Colored pencils
Felt-tip pen: fine point
Sieve: fine mesh for sifting your sand
Sand: 1 cup
Box: a cardboard or wooden cigar box approximately 6 inches by 8 1/2 inches, by 3 inches deep
Cardboard: lightweight, similar to a playing card; one piece, 10 inches by 12 inches
Drawing paper: two pieces, 8 inches by 10 inches
Decorative paper: one piece, 12 inches by 15 inches or enough to cover the sides and back of the box
Trim: gold embossed paper border or braid, 36 inches
Glass: light picture, same size as the outside dimensions of the box
Beads: eight clear glass seed or Indian beads
Nail: one bright common, 2 1/2 inches long
Plastic drinking straw
Wire: 32-gauge brass
White glue

To Make a Leotard Sand Toy

To make the sand wheel (Plate E), trace the two patterns marked "sand wheel sides" on the lightweight cardboard, copying all markings carefully. Cut out the circles and then cut the slots, shown by the solid lines, with a razor

knife. Cut two cardboard sand wheel hubs, and glue one to each sand wheel side on the marked surface, matching the center points. Make small holes through these centers about 1/8 inch in diameter. Cut twelve sand wheel buckets from the cardboard, following the pattern. Score and fold them along the broken lines. Fit the bucket tabs into the slots in the sand wheel sides, as shown in the illustration.

Cut, score, and fold the cardboard bracket (Plate E). Make the hole in the bracket larger than the diameter of the 2 1/2 inch long nail, but not so large that the head of the nail will pass through it. Insert the nail through the hole in the bracket. Cut a 1/8-inch section of straw and thread it on the nail to act as a spacer. Look at the plan, and fit the wheel onto the nail so that the sand will fall onto the short sides of the buckets. See the illustration of the wheel assembly. The wheel should fit tightly so that wheel and nail will revolve together. Add a drop of glue along the nail on each side of the wheel, if necessary. Thread a 3/8-inch straw spacer on the nail, and set the whole thing aside while you make the sand chute.

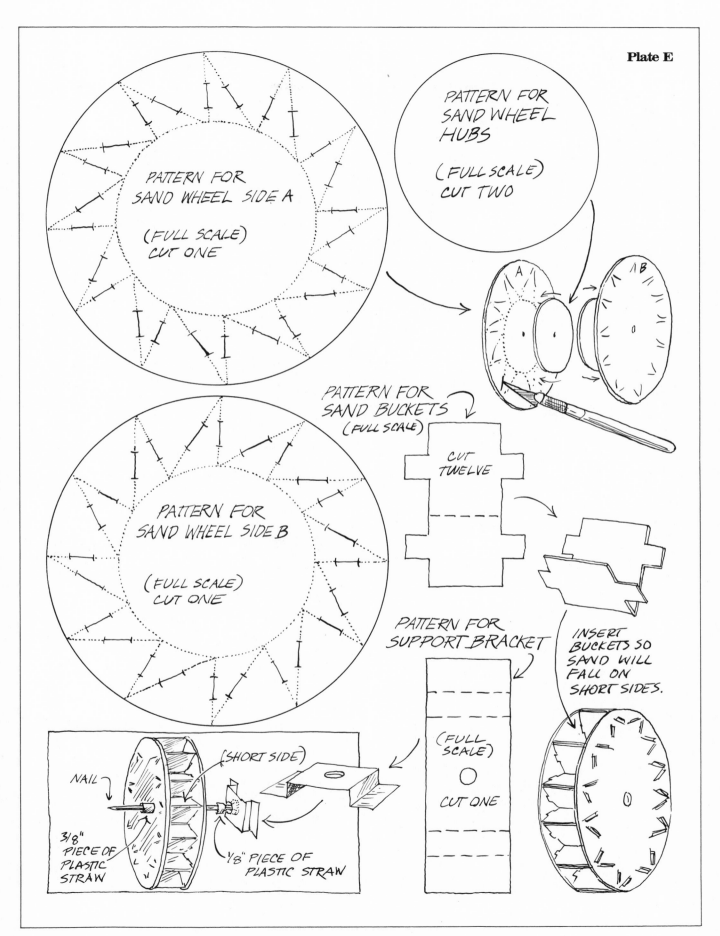

PATTERN FOR
SAND WHEEL SIDE A

(FULL SCALE)
CUT ONE

PATTERN FOR
SAND WHEEL
HUBS

(FULL SCALE)
CUT TWO

A

B

PATTERN FOR
SAND BUCKETS
(FULL SCALE)

CUT
TWELVE

PATTERN FOR
SAND WHEEL SIDE B

(FULL SCALE)
CUT ONE

INSERT
BUCKETS SO
SAND WILL
FALL ON
SHORT SIDES.

PATTERN FOR
SUPPORT BRACKET

(SHORT SIDE)

NAIL

3/8"
PIECE OF
PLASTIC
STRAW

1/8" PIECE OF
PLASTIC STRAW

(FULL
SCALE)

CUT ONE

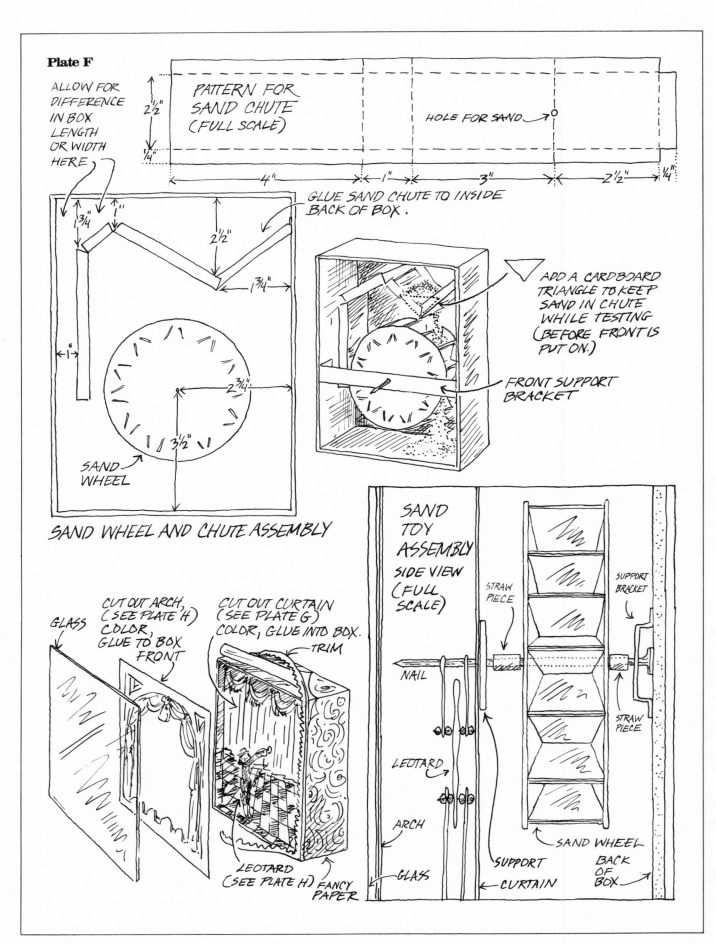

Plate F

ALLOW FOR DIFFERENCE IN BOX LENGTH OR WIDTH HERE

PATTERN FOR SAND CHUTE (FULL SCALE)

2½"

¼"

HOLE FOR SAND →

4" · 1" · 3" · 2½" · ¼"

1¾"

1"

2½"

1¾"

1"

2¾"

3½"

SAND WHEEL

SAND WHEEL AND CHUTE ASSEMBLY

GLUE SAND CHUTE TO INSIDE BACK OF BOX.

ADD A CARDBOARD TRIANGLE TO KEEP SAND IN CHUTE WHILE TESTING (BEFORE FRONT IS PUT ON.)

FRONT SUPPORT BRACKET

GLASS

CUT OUT ARCH, (SEE PLATE 'H') COLOR, GLUE TO BOX FRONT

CUT OUT CURTAIN (SEE PLATE G) COLOR, GLUE INTO BOX.

TRIM

LEOTARD (SEE PLATE H)

FANCY PAPER

SAND TOY ASSEMBLY SIDE VIEW (FULL SCALE)

STRAW PIECE

SUPPORT BRACKET

NAIL

LEOTARD

ARCH

GLASS

SUPPORT

CURTAIN

STRAW PIECE

SAND WHEEL

BACK OF BOX

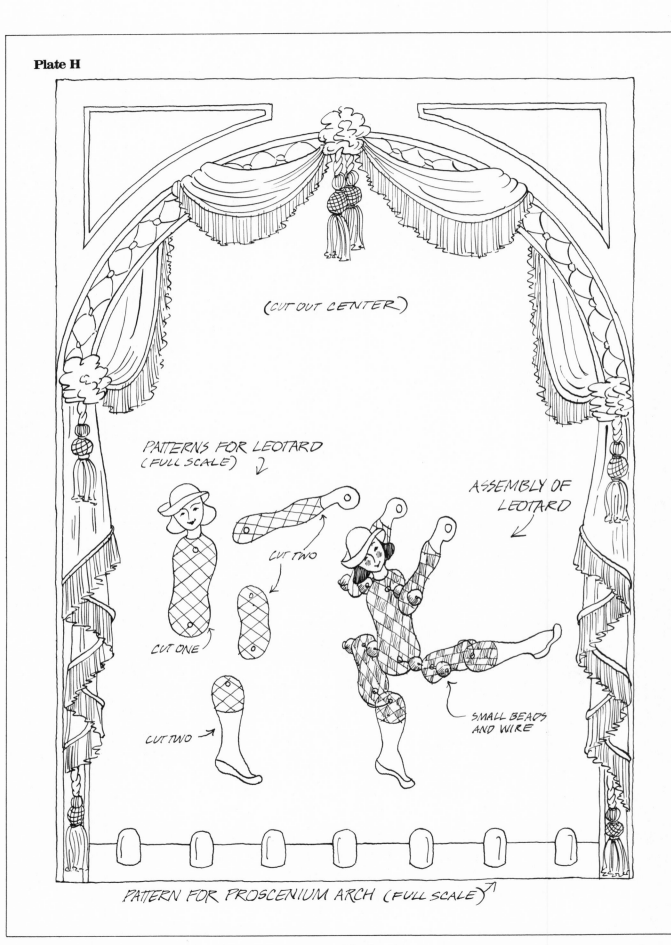

(CUT OUT CENTER)

PATTERNS FOR LEOTARD
(FULL SCALE)

ASSEMBLY OF
LEOTARD

CUT TWO

CUT ONE

CUT TWO

SMALL BEADS
AND WIRE

PATTERN FOR PROSCENIUM ARCH (FULL SCALE)

Cut, score, and bend the chute, as shown in the plan (Plate F). The hole in the chute should be made quite small to start with. You may need to enlarge it later, depending on the size of the sand grains. Glue the sand chute to the back of the box. If your box is slightly larger or smaller than the one specified, make the adjustments in measurements on the top and left-hand sides of the chute. The hole in the sand chute and the sand wheel must be kept in the relationship shown, or will not work.

To install the wheel in the box (Plate F), cut a front support bracket — a 1-inch strip of cardboard as long as the box is wide plus 1 inch. Score and bend a 1/2-inch tab on both ends so that the support just fits inside the width of the box. Make a hole 2 3/4 inches from the right hand side to support the nail wheel axle. Position the wheel as shown and glue the back support bracket to the back of the box. Glue the front support bracket in place. When the glue is dry, test the wheel to make sure that it spins freely and that the nail and wheel still turn together.

Glue a cardboard triangle to the V in the sand chute to form a sand hopper. Sift about a cupful of sand through a fine sieve to remove any oversize grains. Spoon some sand into the hopper and let it trickle through the hole. Enlarge the hole, if necessary, to produce a slow, steady stream of sand.

When the sand flows easily and the wheel turns at a fairly even rate, you are ready to finish the box. Trace the pattern for the backdrop curtain (Plate G), and transfer it to a good grade of drawing paper. Draw in all of the lines with a black, fine felt-tip pen. Try to keep the lines light and clean. If you need to adjust the drawing to the size of the box, this is the time to do it. The backdrop curtain should be exactly the size of the inside measurements of your box plus an additional 1/4 inch for a glueing strip all the way around. Color the curtains a soft, dull red and the fringe gold. Bend the glueing strip forward and fit it into the box. Mark and cut a neat hole where the nail will

come through, making it just large enough so that the nail will not bind.

Lay the box on its back and pour in 3/4 of a cup of sand. Paint the front edges of the sand chute, hopper, and support bracket with glue and press the background curtain against them until they are dry and firmly stuck. Then glue the edges of the backdrop to the sides of the box, making sure that you leave no gaps for sand to escape.

Cut pieces for the Leotard (Plate H) from lightweight cardboard or heavy drawing paper. Draw in his face and clothing with the felt-tip pen and color each diamond of his suit in a different pastel color, using colored pencils. His hat, stockings, face, and arms should be white. Give him bright pink cheeks and black hair and slippers. Pierce holes with a darning needle and string him together with the 32-gauge brass wire and small beads, as spacers. All of his joints should be very loose and flexible. Pierce holes through his hands and slip them onto the nail. Fix them firmly in place with a drop of glue.

Copy the proscenium arch on drawing paper (Plate H). Adjust it, if necessary, so that it is the exact size of the outside dimensions of the box. Draw in the lines with the felt-tip pen and color it. Cut out the center portion, leaving only the curtain and stage lights to frame the stage. Cut, or have cut by a glazier, a piece of light picture glass to the exact outside dimensions of the box. Glue the proscenium arch face down on the glass, using very small dabs of white glue — just enough to hold it in place. Cover the outside of the box with decorative paper and attach the glass to the box with a fine line of glue all the way around the edge. Cover the cut edge of the glass with a border of gold paper or braid.

To start the sand motor, hold the box in an upright position with "Leotard" facing you. Turn the box very slowly to the left in a counterclockwise direction. Make two complete turns. Stand your little stage on a table and watch the show.

PART THREE

STRING POWERED TOYS

Pull Strings on These Things

String toys are some of the oldest of man's playthings, probably only second to the ball in order of antiquity. The most basic of these are the pull toys, and examples still exist that were made before 1100 B.C. A more sophisticated string toy, located in the British Museum, is dated 1100 B.C. It is an Egyptian wooden tiger with a string-operated jaw that opens to bare his bronze fangs.

You may be interested to know that the yo-yo, which seems such a modern toy, is so old that no one knows when or where it originated. There are pictures on ancient Greek vases of people playing with them. Yo-yos were tremendously popular in France in the 1790s and were made in a great variety of materials, from sugar to gold. These toys weren't just for children; the Duke of Orleans was reported to have given a lady friend a diamond-studded model valued at 2,400 *livres*. While we must resist the temptation to claim that the French Revolution was caused by a yo-yo, it is a fact that yo-yos became known throughout Europe by the name *emigrant* or *emigre* because many of the French nobility carried the toys with them in their flight from the guillotine. Yo-yos were called bandilors or quizzes in England, where their popularity lasted well into the nineteenth century. During the last great upsurge of yo-yo mania in the 1960s, a four-pound monster, fifteen inches across, was operated from a tenth story window in New York City.

Another string toy of equal antiquity, variously known as a magic wheel, a buzzer, or a water-cutter may be familiar to you in the form of a two hole button on a loop of string that spins around as you alternately pull on, then relax, the string which twists first one way and then the other. This toy is also depicted on Greek vases. While it probably originated in the Orient, it is common to people all over the world, from New Guinea natives with a stone age culture to Eskimos.

One of the best known of all string operated toys is the marionette. These, too, are very old, but they have never lost the power to charm viewers with their movements. Our miniature wrestlers are an early, simple form of marionette. They require little skill to operate, yet they put on a very good show.

String-started tops have been around for centuries. Plato refers to them in his *Republic*. The Latin word for this type of top is *turbo*. They became popular in England in the fourteenth century and remained one of the most common toys of childhood throughout the Victorian era. Flying tops seem to have been developed in the late 1800s. They were simply a variation on the string-started top, directed upward with the bulbous spinner replaced by a winglike piece of cardboard.

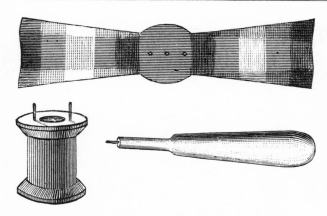

The flying whirligig consists of a spool with two headless nails driven into it and placed on a spindle with another headless nail in the top. The wings are made of cardboard, bent to catch the air and pierced to fit over the three nails. When a string is wound onto the spool and then pulled sharply off, the wings soar into the air like a helicopter.

Boys playing peg-in-the-ring. The object of the game was to hit the other player's top with such force as to break it in two, whereupon the winner took the center peg as a trophy.

"About the beginning of the present century [nineteenth] the bandilor became suddenly a fashionable toy under the name of Quiz, and scarcely any person of fashion was without one of these toys."

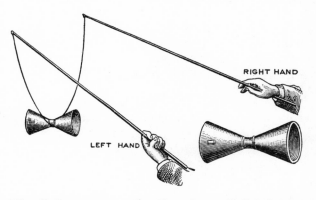

RIGHT HAND

LEFT HAND

The flying cone or devil on two sticks, known in France as le diable, was so popular that "the sport was not confined to children, but ladies and even persons of great eminence strove to excel in it, often to the great risk of the glass and porcelain in parlors."

The whip top (left) is made to spin faster by lashing it with an eel-skin whip. The peg top (right) is operated by winding a string around the body of the top and then throwing it with great force from above the head. These tops were made of extremely hard and heavy wood such as box ebony or lignum vitae.

The water-cutter is made of a 3-inch piece of tin cut in the shape of a star with two holes in it, 1 1/2 inches apart. A string is then looped through the holes and tied. "If spun over a basin of water, and allowed to dip in as it spins, it cuts through the water and sends a shower of spray from it over the operator when it spins in one direction, and over the spectators when it spins in the other."

WRESTLERS

These miniature wrestlers put on a convincing fight. Operated in a dimly lit room, or on a marionette stage with a dark background, they seem to be animated by some hidden power and will perform in a most amusing way. The more realistically they are carved, the better the illusion. Even if they are cut from flat pieces of wood or cardboard, they will delight and mystify those not in on the secret. Stringed figures like these are some of the most ancient of moving toys. A twelfth-century manuscript in the Paris Library shows two people playing with two knights in armor made in much the same way.

Tools and Materials

Needle-nose pliers
Knife: sharp paring or jackknife
Drill: with a 1/16-inch bit
Paintbrushes: small artist's
Sandpaper: fine
Wire: 20-gauge, 16 inches
Balsa wood: four pieces, 3 inches by 2 inches by 4 inches; one piece, 1 1/2 inches by 2 inches by 4 inches; one piece, 1 inch by 2 inches by 4 inches
Paint: artist's acrylic or model
Primer sealer
Leather: one, 1- by 1/2-inch piece of chamois or other pliable leather
White glue
Thread: button and carpet, black

To Build the Wrestlers

Trace the patterns for all of the parts (Plate A) and cut them out of paper. Arrange them on the blocks of balsa so that you can fit the two heads on the 1 1/2- by 2- by 4-inch piece, the two arms on the 1- by 2- by 4-inch piece, the two legs on each of the two 3- by 2- by 4-inch pieces, and one body on each of the two remaining 3- by 2- by 4-inch pieces. Trace the outlines of the fronts and backs on either side of the wood block. Then trace the side views, making sure the side views are properly reversed so that heads and feet are pointing in the right directions.

Using these guidelines and frequently comparing your work with the patterns, carefully carve out the various pieces. When they are done, drill 1/16-inch holes straight through the bodies at the shoulders and hips and through the arms and legs, as indicated. Wire the figures together and test them to make sure that the arms and legs move freely.

Take them apart again and sand all the parts until smooth. Give them a coat of white primer sealer and let them dry. Now paint the figures. The wrestlers' jerseys and caps usually have red and white stripes. Their knee breeches, blue, their stockings, white, and their shoes and belts, black. Or use your own color combinations. Paint their arms and faces a flesh color, and give one black hair and the other brown, so you can tell them apart.

When the paint is dry (Plate B), wire the arms and legs to the bodies, making small unobtrusive loops of wire at shoulders and hips. Cut two pieces of leather about 1/4 inch by 3/8 inch and glue one end of one into the notch on the body side of the neck and the other end of that one into the notch on the head side of the neck so that the head will nod slightly. Do the same for the other wrestler.

To operate, run an 8-foot length of heavy black thread through the hole at the center of the arms. Tie one end of the string to a chair rung about 6 inches from the floor and hold the other end in your hand. With the figures midway between you and the chair, twitch the string and the wrestlers will start to perform. You stimulate their antics by small movements of the string.

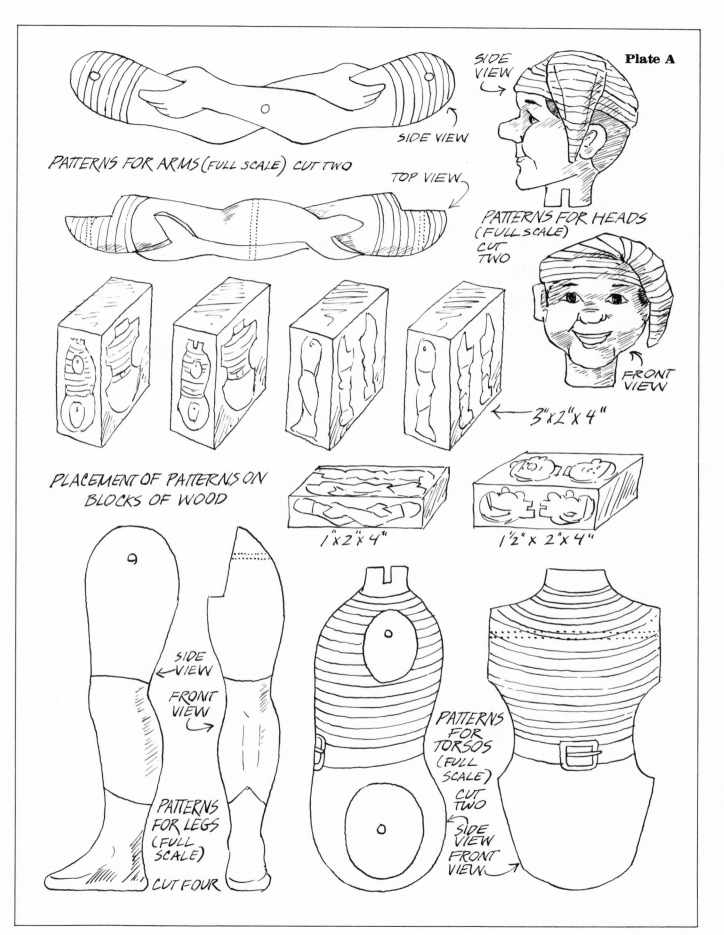

SIDE VIEW

Plate A

PATTERNS FOR ARMS (FULL SCALE) CUT TWO

SIDE VIEW

TOP VIEW

PATTERNS FOR HEADS (FULL SCALE) CUT TWO

FRONT VIEW

PLACEMENT OF PATTERNS ON BLOCKS OF WOOD

3"x 2"x 4"

1"x 2"x 4"

1½" x 2"x 4"

SIDE VIEW

FRONT VIEW

PATTERNS FOR LEGS (FULL SCALE)

CUT FOUR

PATTERNS FOR TORSOS (FULL SCALE) CUT TWO

SIDE VIEW

FRONT VIEW

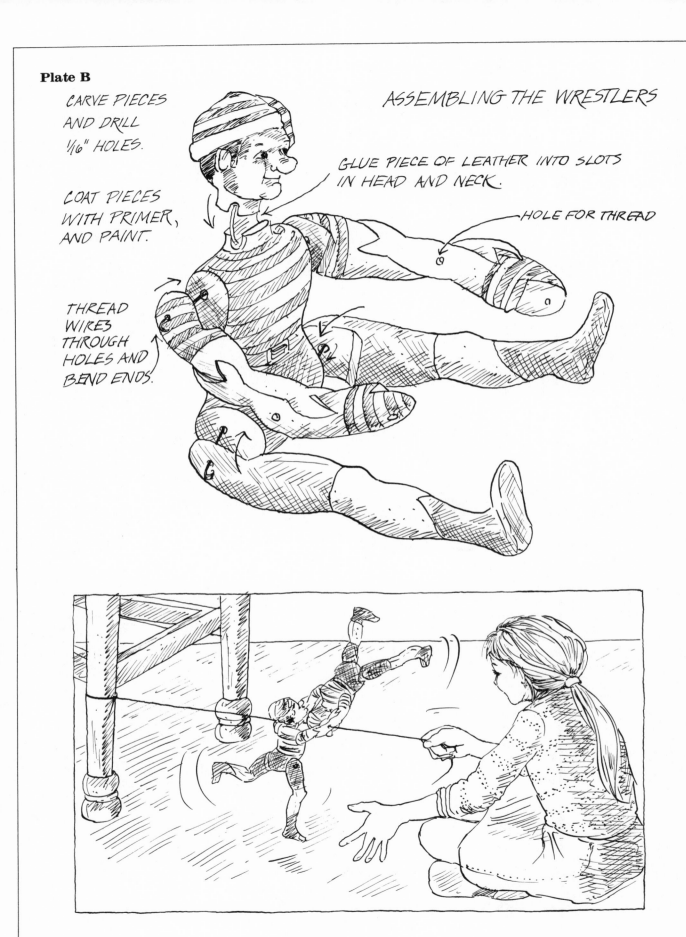

Plate B

CARVE PIECES AND DRILL 1/16" HOLES.

COAT PIECES WITH PRIMER, AND PAINT.

THREAD WIRES THROUGH HOLES AND BEND ENDS.

ASSEMBLING THE WRESTLERS

GLUE PIECE OF LEATHER INTO SLOTS IN HEAD AND NECK.

HOLE FOR THREAD

THE CAT THAT RUNS UPHILL

This almost life-size cat puts on a surprising show. It can be an indoor toy for one person to make and enjoy, or it can be an outdoor toy for two. The mechanism is really quite simple and consists of a small box fitted inside with four spools through which two long strings are threaded. The strings are held or fastened close together at one end. When the strings are jerked sharply apart at the other end, the box will travel along the strings at a great rate — even uphill. If nylon cord is used, the cat makes a very satisfactory squealing noise.

Tools and Materials

Drill: with a 1/4-inch bit
Razor knife
Scissors
Coping saw
Box: about 4 inches by 5 inches, by 1 3/4 inches deep, can be sturdy cardboard or wood
Spools: four wood or plastic sewing-thread spools, slightly shorter than the depth of the box
Doweling: 1/4-inch diameter, 12 inches long
Cardboard: two pieces, 10 by 14 inches
Paints: artist's acrylic or colored pencils
White glue
String: strong and lightweight, twice as long as you want your cat to travel, but 20 feet at least
Washers: eight metal 7/8-inch washers with 3/8-inch center holes
Beads: four large wooden

To Build a Cat That Runs Uphill

To make the spool box mechanism (Plate C), drill or cut four 1/4-inch holes in the top and bottom of the box near the corners and 1 1/4 inches from each side. Be sure the holes are exactly parallel to each other. Cut a 1/4-inch wide slit in each end of the box, as shown. Cut four pieces of doweling 1/4 inch longer than the depth of the box measured from the outside. Slip a spool onto each piece of doweling. If the spool will not spin freely, sand the doweling down until it does. Slip a washer on either side of the spool, and insert one end of the dowels into the holes in the bottom of the box. Close the lid of the box so the dowels go through the holes in the lid. Thread two long strings through the box as shown.

Test the mechanism to see if it works. Tie the two front strings together and tack them to the top of a door. Take the box to the far end of the room. The strings should be at least that long. Hold one string in each hand and pull both taut. Suddenly jerk your hands wide apart, one up and one down, and the box will shoot up the string. Be careful to have the strings untwisted before you pull them apart.

When all is working properly, you can decorate the box. Trace the cat pattern onto the cardboard (Plates C and D). Reverse the pattern so there is a back and a front. Make the right side with only right legs, and the left side with left legs. Paint the cat in as furry a manner as possible and glue it to the sides of the box. Tie a large wooden bead at the end of each string, so they can't be pulled out of the box.

Two people can play this in another manner. Each person takes turns holding the strings together at one end and jerking the strings apart. Then the cat can travel back and forth between them.

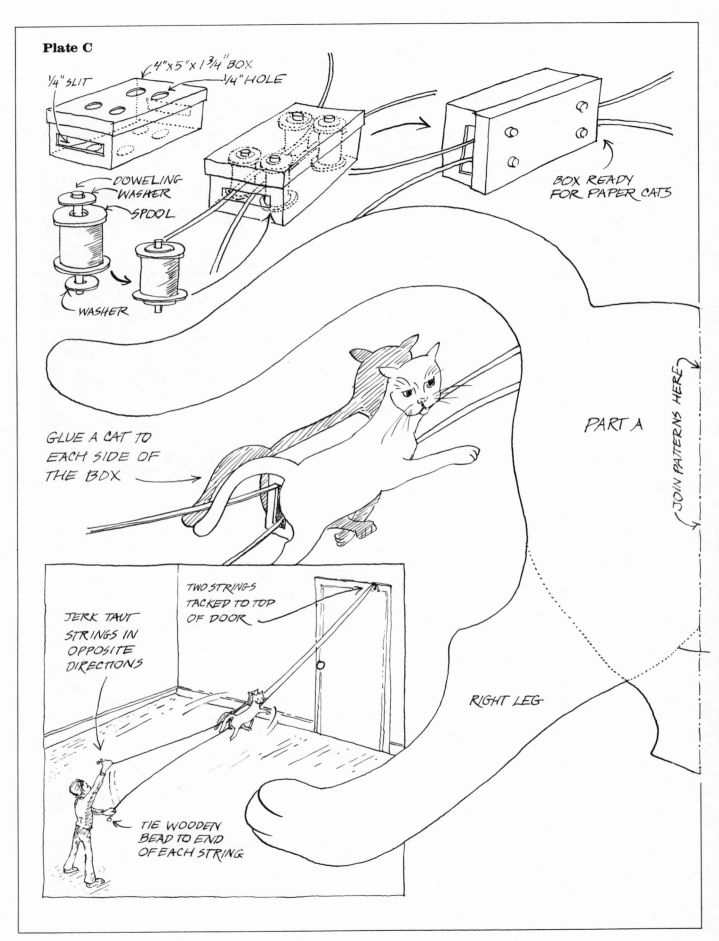

Plate C

1/4" SLIT

4"x5"x1 3/4" BOX

1/4" HOLE

DOWELING

WASHER

SPOOL

WASHER

BOX READY FOR PAPER CATS

GLUE A CAT TO EACH SIDE OF THE BOX

PART A

JOIN PATTERNS HERE

TWO STRINGS TACKED TO TOP OF DOOR

JERK TAUT STRINGS IN OPPOSITE DIRECTIONS

RIGHT LEG

TIE WOODEN BEAD TO END OF EACH STRING

Plate D

CUT TWO CAT PATTERNS,
DRAW FACE ON ONLY ONE.

A B

RIGHT LEG

RIGHT LEG

A B

LEFT LEG

LEFT LEG

JOIN PATTERNS HERE

PART B

PATTERN FOR CAT
(FULL SCALE)

RIGHT LEG

LEFT LEG

LEFT LEG

AN AIRPLANE TO CARRY MESSAGES

This is an interesting variation of The Cat That Runs Uphill. It is an airplane built around the same spool mechanism. (See page 65 for materials and directions.) The matchbox on top of the plane carries mail or messages. Tack one end of the two strings to an upstairs window frame. Pull the upper string taut and tie it to the top of a post in the backyard. A quick jerk on the untied lower string will send the airplane zipping up to someone waiting in the upstairs window.

Tools and Materials

Razor knife
Scissors
Needle-nose pliers
Paintbrush: small
Cardboard: lightweight
Construction paper
Beads: four, 3/8-inch with large holes
Wire: 18-gauge
White glue
Plastic drinking straws
Matchbox: small size
Paint: model or artist's acrylic

To Build an Airplane to Carry Messages

Trace the patterns (Plates E, F, and G) for the fuselage, wings, and tails on cardboard and cut out. You will need two of each. Decorate them as you wish. Make the same spool-box mechanism as for The Cat That Runs Uphill. Glue the fuselage, wings, and tails to the box. Then glue the matchbox to the top of the box.

Cut two propellers of construction paper following the pattern (Plate F). Glue the points A, B, C, and D to point E. Make a small hole at point E through all layers. Assemble the propellers as follows: twist a small loop in one end of a straight 7-inch piece of wire, slip on one bead, then a propeller, a second bead, then a 5 1/4-inch length of straw. Finish with a third bead and twist another loop in the wire to hold them all together. Tape the straw to the underside of the wing, along the dotted lines. Repeat for the second propeller. Now you are ready to decide what kind of a plane you've made and paint it up in style.

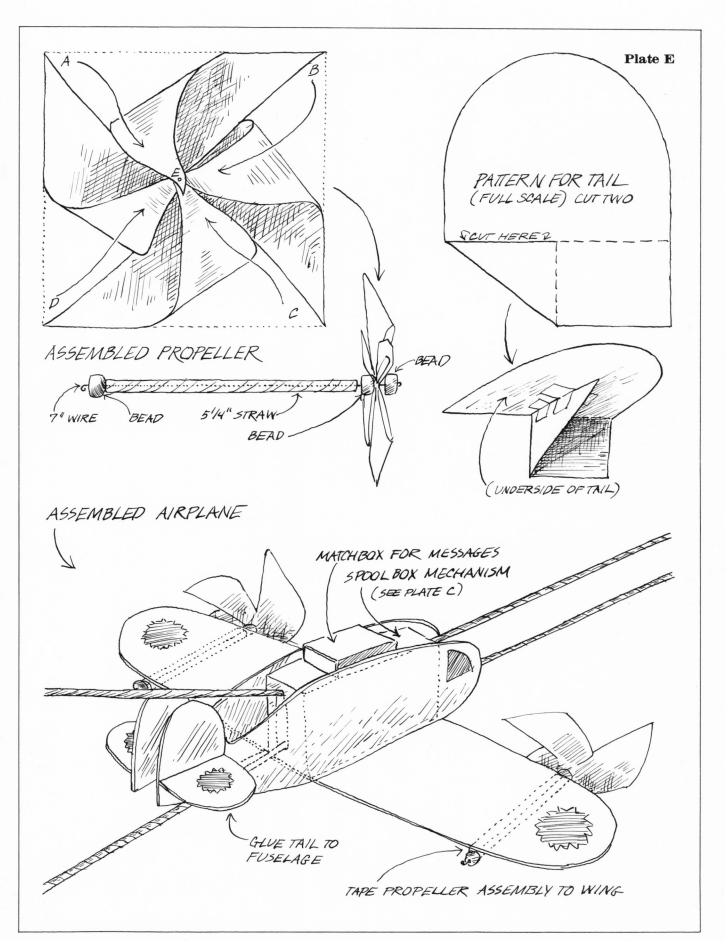

A   B

D   C

ASSEMBLED PROPELLER

7" WIRE   BEAD   5 1/4" STRAW

BEAD

BEAD

PATTERN FOR TAIL
(FULL SCALE) CUT TWO

CUT HERE

(UNDERSIDE OF TAIL)

ASSEMBLED AIRPLANE

MATCHBOX FOR MESSAGES
SPOOL BOX MECHANISM
(SEE PLATE C)

GLUE TAIL TO
FUSELAGE

TAPE PROPELLER ASSEMBLY TO WING

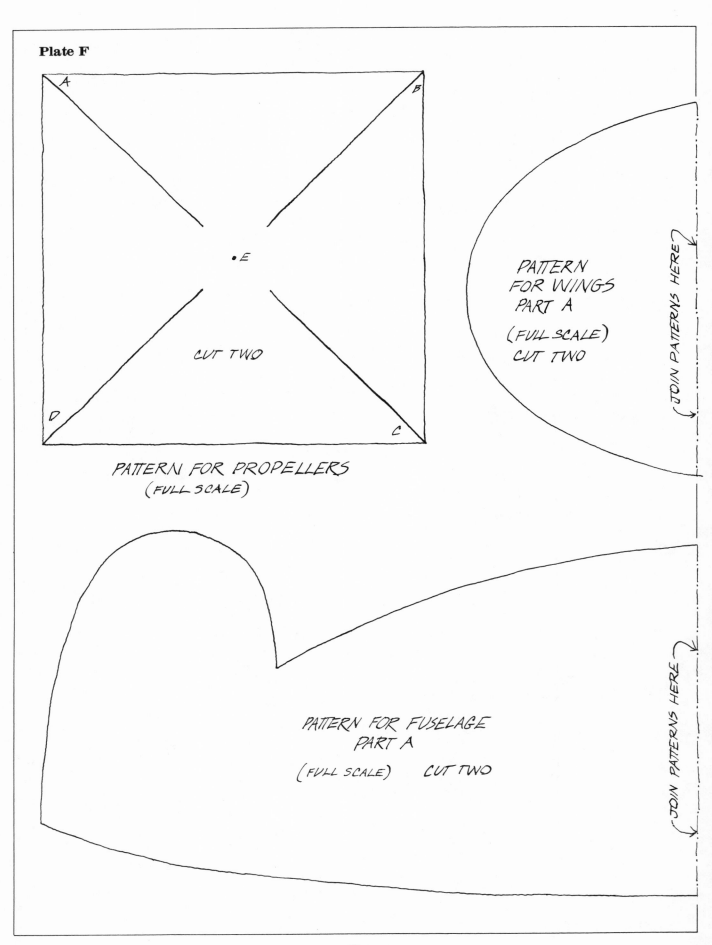

A
B
• E
D
C

CUT TWO

PATTERN FOR PROPELLERS
(FULL SCALE)

PATTERN
FOR WINGS
PART A
(FULL SCALE)
CUT TWO

(JOIN PATTERNS HERE)

PATTERN FOR FUSELAGE
PART A
(FULL SCALE)   CUT TWO

(JOIN PATTERNS HERE)

Plate G

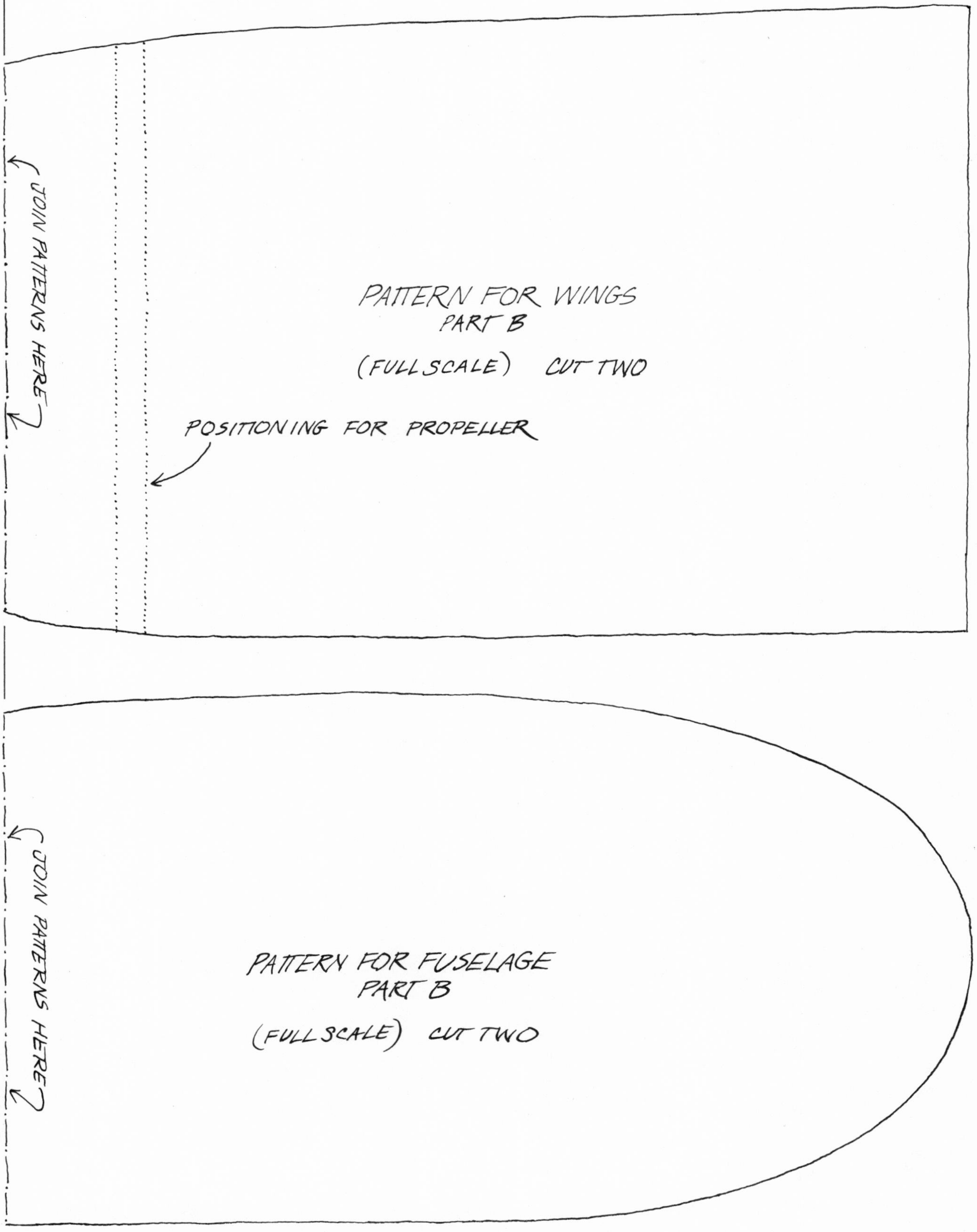
JOIN PATTERNS HERE
PATTERN FOR WINGS
PART B
(FULL SCALE) CUT TWO
POSITIONING FOR PROPELLER
JOIN PATTERNS HERE
PATTERN FOR FUSELAGE
PART B
(FULL SCALE) CUT TWO

PART FOUR

WIND POWERED TOYS

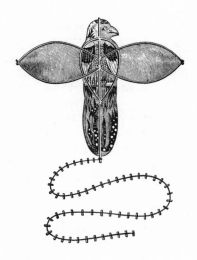

Designed to Catch and Go

George R. Mortimer becalmed at Lake Hopatcong, New Jersey, in 1931.

There is something wonderfully exciting about the wind. Nothing gives quite the same feeling of exhilaration and power that you get from a kite pulling hard in a bright spring sky or a boat coming to life as a summer breeze fills its sails. One of the best things about the wind is that it is free and available to all. You can easily put it to work for you, whether you are building toys or doing something more practical. For centuries man has used the wind to grind flour, pump water, and send ships across the seas; today it is being used to generate electricity.

The first really efficient wind machines were ships, so it isn't surprising that even in ancient times there were attempts to use sails for propelling vehicles on land. Probably the most successful was the railway sail car, and we've included plans for a working model that you can build.

One of the oddest wind-blown designs was George Pocock's "Charvolant," or flying car, built in 1827. It was a light carriage drawn by kites. This sounds highly impractical, but *The Boy's Own Book* of 1853 tells us that "the Master of a respectable academy at Bristol has lately succeeded in traveling along the public roads, (we believe from Bristol to London,) with amazing speed, in the most safe and accurate manner

possible, not withstanding the variation in the wind and the crookedness of the road."

Much more successful than any of the land sailers were the iceboats that appeared in the eighteenth century. It didn't take long to translate this idea into a sport for the daring. The first known American iceboat was built in 1790. Before long, iceboating was popular on harbors, lakes, and streams throughout the northern United States and Canada. By the mid-nineteenth century many of the how-to books for young people gave plans for home-built "Tom Thumb" iceboats.

Skate sailing was another wind-powered sport for the adventurous. It grew from the idea of spreading your coat to catch the wind, something skaters had been doing for a long time. "Every Boy His Own Iceboat" was an article written for *St. Nicholas Magazine* by Charles Norton; in it he described his own invention, an elaborate double-sailed rig that had the advantage of allowing the skater to see where he was going. Other arrangements presented problems; with the Norwegian rig, one skater had to be the "mast" and hold the sail, trusting to Providence and his crewmate — the steersman — because the sail completely blocked his view. Later sails for skaters had isinglass or plastic windows so they could see what was ahead.

The Norton Rig for skate sailing

These boys aren't content to stand around and just wait for something to happen. They're off to test a new kite.

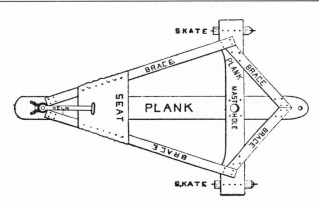

Plan for a "Tom Thumb" iceboat. Some models used the rear skate as a rudder; in others the sailor wore skates and steered with his feet.

An ancient sail car built and rigged like a ship.

An iceboat being helped over a crack in the ice. Unexpected holes in the ice are a major hazard.

Iceboats on the Hudson River in the 1880s.

MODEL ICE SCHOONER

Iceboats originated in the Netherlands during the eighteenth century. The earliest North American example was a wooden box with three runners and a spritsail. It was built by Oliver Booth at Poughkeepsie, New York, in 1790.

Iceboats appeal to the daring. They are very fast, and in the hands of a good sailor, they can travel three or four times faster than the speed of the wind. In 1908, Commodore Elisha Price's lateen-rigged "Clarel" was clocked at 140 mph. This was the fastest that man had traveled at that time. It still is very fast, considering the rider is on an open rig, on the ice.

A small and very much simplified version of the iceboat can be put together and rigged in a few hours. You can probably find enough scrap lumber around the house to build more than one. They are competitive racers, and when you get cold standing around and watching them perform, see if you can keep up with them on skates. We bet you can't!

Tools and Materials

Tin snips
Hammer
Saw
Needle and carpet thread
Wood molding: 3/8 inch by 1 1/2 inch — one piece, 2 feet long and two pieces, 1 foot long; 1/2-inch quarter round — two pieces, 1 foot long and two pieces, 15 inches long
Paintbrush: small
Wood blocks: 1-inch by 2-inch stock — two pieces, 2 inches long
Tin: four pieces, 2 inches by 3 inches, cut from a tin can
Sandpaper
Nails
Brads: 1/2-inch
Tacks: 1/4-inch carpet
White glue
Fabric: lightweight cotton; one piece, 12 inches by 24 inches
Wire: 22-gauge
Paint: enamel

To Build an Ice Schooner

To make the frame, cut and sand the wood blocks and molding to the dimensions given. Glue and nail the crosspieces to the body, as shown in the plan. Glue and nail (with small brads) the masts, made from the 12-inch pieces of quarter round, to the two blocks. Then glue and nail the blocks to the body, directly over the crosspieces.

To make the blades, cut four 2- by 3-inch pieces of tin. Bend them down the middle the long way into 90-degree angles. Tack the blades to the crosspieces, as shown. Paint the frame and the quarter-round spars and masts.

To make the sails, measure and cut the fabric following the sail plans. Notice that they are for the finished size, so you must add enough for 1/2-inch hems all around. Turn and sew the hems along the 13 1/2-inch side and the 10 3/8-inch side. Turn under the hem on the 15-inch side and lace it to the spar with a darning needle and carpet thread. The spars are the two 15-inch lengths of quarter-round molding. Sew a loose loop of carpet thread through the sail and around the mast; tie it as shown in the sail plans.

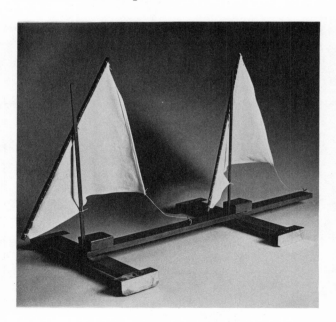

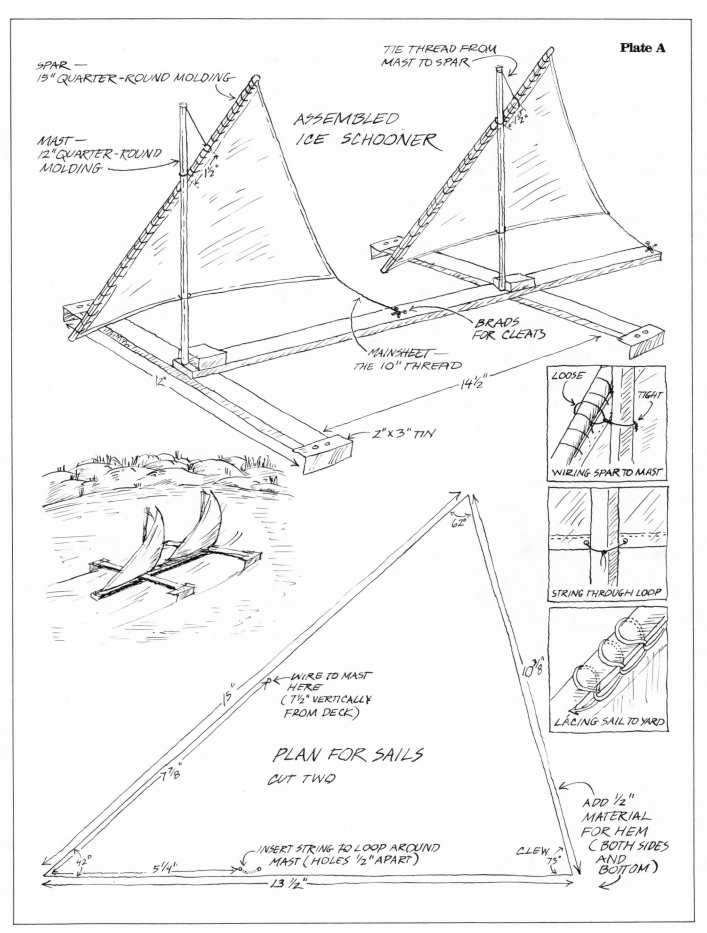

SPAR —
15" QUARTER-ROUND MOLDING

TIE THREAD FROM
MAST TO SPAR

ASSEMBLED
ICE SCHOONER

MAST —
12" QUARTER-ROUND
MOLDING

1½"

1½"

BRADS
FOR CLEATS

MAINSHEET —
THE 10" THREAD

12"

14½"

2"x 3" TIN

LOOSE   TIGHT

WIRING SPAR TO MAST

STRING THROUGH LOOP

LACING SAIL TO YARD

62°

10⅜"

WIRE TO MAST
HERE
(7½" VERTICALLY
FROM DECK)

15"

7⅞"

PLAN FOR SAILS
CUT TWO

ADD ½"
MATERIAL
FOR HEM
(BOTH SIDES
AND
BOTTOM)

INSERT STRING TO LOOP AROUND
MAST (HOLES ½" APART)

42°

5¼"

13½"

CLEW
75°

BIG FISH—LITTLE FISH KITE

Every book on toys published before 1900 featured this kite design and a wonderful variety of ways to decorate it. We decided that one hundred thousand English schoolboys couldn't be wrong, that it was high time to revive the bow-top kite. The original directions called for half of a hoop, shaved down to make it lighter. Undoubtedly the waning popularity of the hoop as a plaything hastened the demise of the traditional bow-top kite.

The old directions called for a string tail fifteen times the length of the kite with strips of paper tied on every 6 inches. Our best source, however, advised against this as "it reminds one rather of curl-papers than of anything else, and they are continually becoming inextricably entangled with each other," and recommended an equally long string with only a tassel or some appropriate figure tied at the end. (In case you don't remember, ladies once set curls in their hair by tying them up with pieces of paper, called curl papers.)

Tools and Materials

Knife: paring or jackknife
Coping saw
Drill: with a 1/8-inch bit
Scissors
Needle-nose pliers
White glue
Strong cotton cord
Wire: 22-gauge
Flat screen molding: 1/4 inch by 3/4 inch, 60 inches long

Quarter-round molding: 1/4 inch, one piece, 60 inches long; two pieces, 24 inches long; and one piece, 7 inches long
Paper: 36 inches by 72 inches
Paint: enamel or artist's acrylic
Masking tape

To Build a Big Fish Kite

To make the frame of the kite, shape one end of the 60-inch screen molding into a graceful point with a knife. Following the diagram, cut 1/8-inch notches on both sides of the molding: at point D, 2 inches from the top, and at point E, 19 inches from the bottom. Cut a 1/2-inch slit in the end of the molding at F. Drill 1/8-inch holes through the molding at points H and G.

Mark the exact center of the 60-inch length of quarter-round molding. Cut shallow notches which go all around the molding, 1/2 inch from each end at points A and C. This will form the bow of the kite. Experiment with bending it gently into a half circle. It will bend most easily if the rounded surface of the molding is on the outside of the curve. Center the bow piece at point D on the upright and wire it there securely. Tie a long piece of strong cord to the bow at point A; take the cord around the upright at point B, and knot it so that point A is 19 1/2 inches from point B. Take a loop around the bow at point C and pull the cord in, gently easing the frame top into a perfect half circle. Check to see that the distances from A to B and B to C are equal. Now take the cord to point D, make a loop around the upright, and tie it at point A again. Check the lengths C to D and D to A to make sure they are equal. Take the cord from points A to F through the slit and tie it again at point C. From point C take it to point E where it is tied, then to point A where it is tied and cut. The flying ability of the kite does not depend on the dimensions so much as it does on the balance and symmetry of construction, so do not feel limited to the exact measurements given here.

To cover the kite frame, lay it down on paper. If you cannot find a large enough sheet of paper, glue several sheets together. Trace around the outside of the kite frame with a pencil, adding an additional 3 inches on all sides as a glueing strip; then cut out the paper.

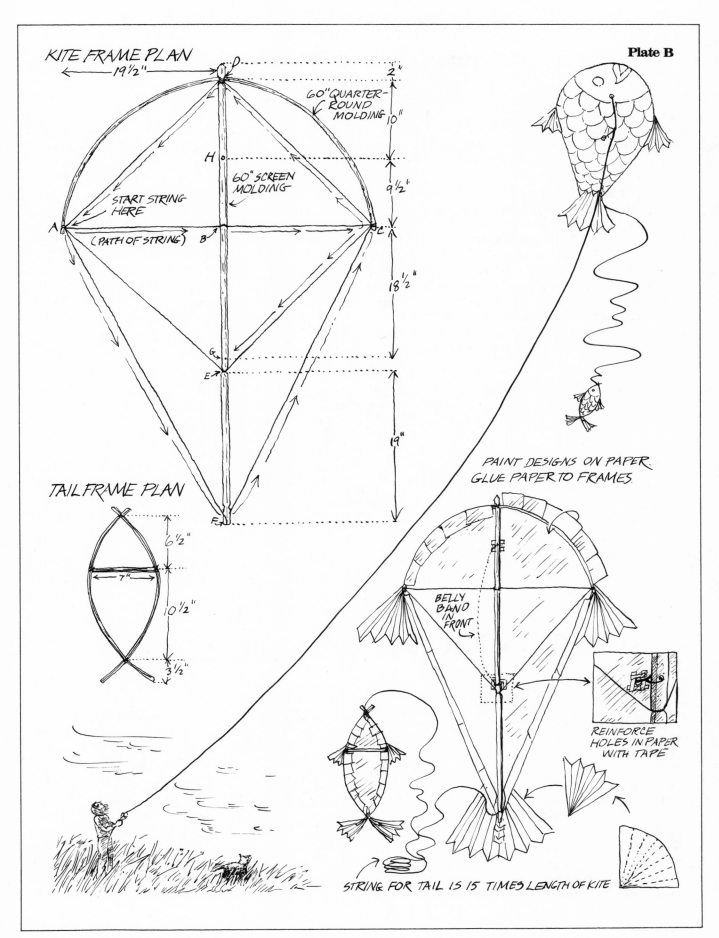

KITE FRAME PLAN

← 19½" →

2"

60" QUARTER-ROUND MOLDING

10"

H

60" SCREEN MOLDING

9½"

START STRING HERE

A

(PATH OF STRING)   B

C

18½"

G

E

19"

F

TAIL FRAME PLAN

6½"

7"

10½"

3½"

PAINT DESIGNS ON PAPER. GLUE PAPER TO FRAMES.

BELLY BAND IN FRONT

REINFORCE HOLES IN PAPER WITH TAPE

STRING FOR TAIL IS 15 TIMES LENGTH OF KITE

Draw in the desired decorations and paint them. We used oil paints because they are not affected by moisture, and they add more body to the paper. Our 1871 source tells us "to remember that as the effect is to be produced from a distance, only the most staring and brilliant colors can be employed, and that fine and finished details will be of no use whatever."

Lay the kite frame on the unpainted side of the paper. Cut the paper to fit around the pointed end of the upright and reinforce around this cut with masking tape. Fold the 3-inch glueing flap over the outer strings and bow; glue securely all around. Reinforce the paper with masking tape at points G and H and make holes through the reinforcing tape to correspond to the holes in the upright.

To make the belly band, thread a 48-inch length of cord through the holes in the upright and the paper, and tie. Add paper fins and a tail, if you like, at points A, C, and F. These are simply quarter circles of paper, folded like a fan and glued in place. They can be a contrasting bright color.

To make the Little Fish Kite tail, wire two 24-inch pieces of quarter-round molding together, as shown in the diagram. Wire in the 7-inch separator. Cover the frame with paper in the same manner as you did the Big Fish. The Little Fish could be cut out of cardboard and painted, if you so desire; or a simple paper tassel fixed to the end of the tail string will work instead. Tie the kite string to the belly band, and your flying fish are ready to soar.

Our fish design is by no means the only possibility for decorating a bow-top kite. The variety and fanciful designs of these Victorian kites should help to stimulate your own imagination.

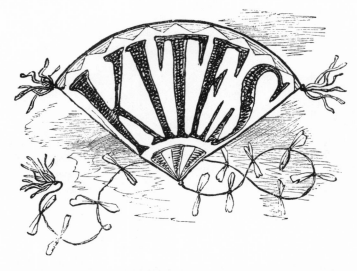

Some Further Ideas on Kite Design

Kites are fun to make and fly. The more elaborate and fanciful their design, the more of a pleasure they are to watch. Kite making used to be one of the most popular spring activities, probably with good cause. Most of our Victorian sources caution the reader that "those which are bought are not always those which fly best; indeed, too often they are made to sell, and don't fly at all."

We've already described how to make the traditional bow-top kite. Here are some of the most popular ways to decorate it, as well as some other shapes favored for kites.

A bearskin rug and a balloon. Tassels of some kind were a traditional part of kite design; here they become paws and flags. They don't do much to improve flying ability, but they do add to the decorative possibilities.

Officers with bright red jackets and blue trousers had lots of gold braid and gold tassel epaulets.

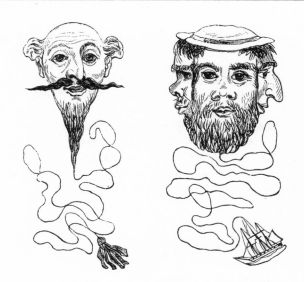

A caricature of Napoleon III and three not-so-jolly tars, with appropriate tail figures.

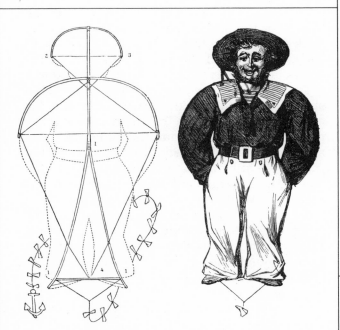

Here's a very jolly tar [seaman], obviously three sheets to the wind. This is a variation of the bow-top kite that can be used for a variety of figures.

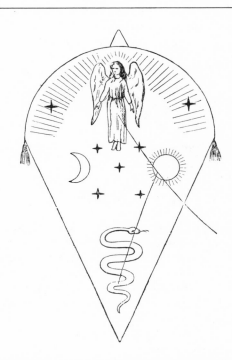

An allegorical device representing the sun, moon, and stars, with an angel flying overhead and a serpent crawling beneath.

Kite tails sometimes had a series of small cloth buckets sewed on that worked like sea anchors. You could put pebbles in them for extra weight instead of making an addition to the length of the tail.

TIGHTROPE WALKER KITE CLIMBER

Kite climbers add a whole new dimension to kite flying. You have the fun of launching your kite and the added pleasure of sending it messages. This intrepid tightrope walker is a lot more interesting than the traditional square of paper blowing up the string. He climbs the kite string backwards and seems about to fall at any minute.

Tools and Materials

Drill: with a 1/8-inch bit
Needle-nose pliers
Razor knife
Coping saw
Scissors
Paintbrush
Bamboo garden stakes: four pieces, 31 inches; one piece, 14 inches; one piece, 7 1/2 inches
Wrapping paper: 36 inches by 36 inches
String
Spools: two large size, sewing-thread spools
Cardboard: lightweight, 8 inches by 16 inches
Paint: artist's acrylic or enamel
Tissue paper: two colors
Bag: small fabric or plastic
Wire: 22-gauge
Masking tape

To Build a Tightrope Walker

To make the frame of the kite climber, you will need bamboo pieces that are very light without being too flexible. Garden stakes that measure about 1/4 inch in diameter at the large end should work right. If you can only find the heavier stakes, split them. Drill a 1/8-inch hole in one of the 31-inch stakes, 7 inches from one end (point J) and another hole 1/2 inch from the bottom (point K). In the other 31-inch stick, cut grooves 6 inches in from either end. This is the horizontal crosspiece.

Saw 1/2-inch slits in the ends of all sticks. Arrange crosspieces according to the frame plan. Bind them all tightly to the main upright with wire. Stretch strings around the frame as shown, fastening the ends of each stick in place by running the string through the slits, then wrapping the string several times around the end of the sticks.

To cover the kite climber, lay the frame on a piece of wrapping paper and trace the outline,
adding a 2-inch border to the outline. Cut out the paper and paint whatever figure you want. Let the paint dry and attach the paper figure to the frame by folding the borders over the strings and the horizontal stick and glueing it all around. Make the face by folding the 8- by 16-inch cardboard in half to make a square. Cut away the corners to make a rounded shape, but leave 4 inches of the fold uncut at the top. Paint the face and hairline on one side, keeping the folded edge at the top of the head. Paint the opposite side the hair color. Open up the fold and tape the top of the vertical framework stick to the inside back of the head. Glue the face down over the other side of the stick.

To make the balancing mechanism, use two more 31-inch bamboo sticks. Drill six 1/8-inch holes in the horizontal stick and three in the angled stick as shown in the drilling plan. Saw a 1/4-inch slit in the end of the horizontal stick. Wire two large spools to the horizontal stick using holes B-C and E-F. Attach the horizontal balancing stick by wiring hole A to the foot of the climber at K. Wire hole G on the angled stick to hole J on the climber; then wire the two balancing sticks to each other at points H and D. Attach a guy string to the end of one of the Tightrope Walker's arms, carry it through the slit in the end of the horizontal balancing stick and back to the other arm of the Tightrope Walker. Pull the string taut so that the figure is perfectly balanced and tie it to itself.

To balance your kite climber, thread a string (to imitate a kite string) through the two spools, and stretch the string between two posts and tie it. The string should be taut, like a clothesline. Tie the small bag to the end of the angled stick at point I. Add pebbles to the bag until its weight is just enough to hold the Tightrope Walker upright.

Cut two 12-inch lengths of wire from coat hangers. Wire these onto the Walker's hands. Then cut two tissue-paper flags and glue the ends around the wires to make flags, as shown. Add another pebble if the flags affect the balance.

Now your climber is ready to walk the wire. Thread the actual kite string through the spools so the Tightrope Walker is facing towards you. Push him off and watch the wind carry him up the string, teetering precariously as he goes.

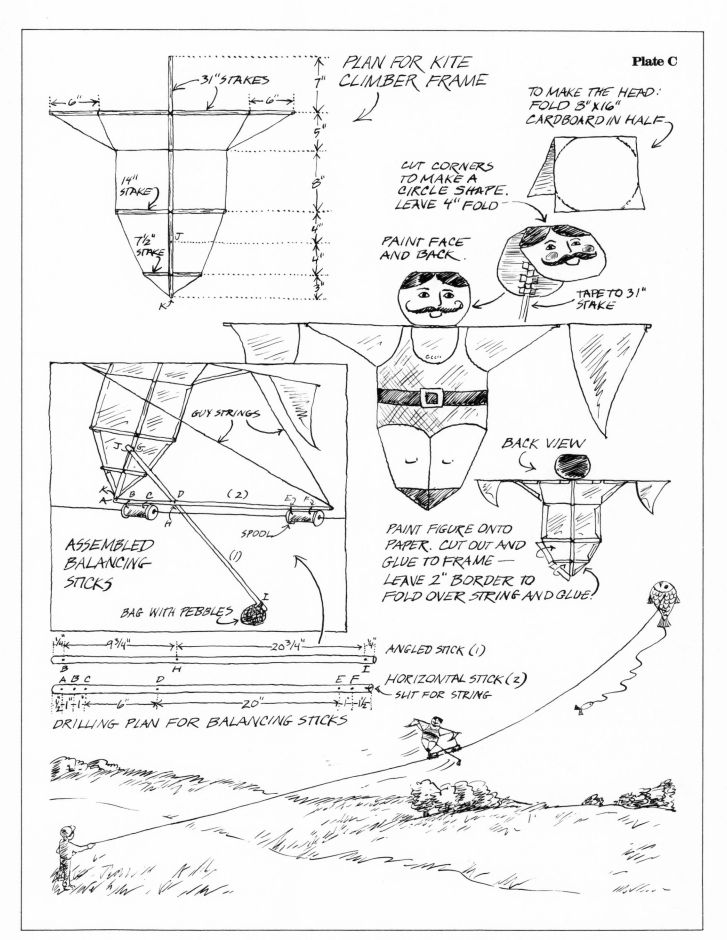

PLAN FOR KITE CLIMBER FRAME

Plate C

31" STAKES

7"

6"   6"

5"

14" STAKE

8"

7½" STAKE

J

4"

4"

3"

K

TO MAKE THE HEAD: FOLD 8"×16" CARDBOARD IN HALF

CUT CORNERS TO MAKE A CIRCLE SHAPE. LEAVE 4" FOLD

PAINT FACE AND BACK.

TAPE TO 31" STAKE

BACK VIEW

PAINT FIGURE ONTO PAPER. CUT OUT AND GLUE TO FRAME — LEAVE 2" BORDER TO FOLD OVER STRING AND GLUE!

GUY STRINGS

J   G

K   B C   D   (2)   E   F
A
         H
                    SPOOL

ASSEMBLED BALANCING STICKS

(1)

BAG WITH PEBBLES

I

¼"   9¾"   20¾"   ¼"
B   H   I
ANGLED STICK (1)

A B C   D   E F
HORIZONTAL STICK (2)
SLIT FOR STRING
½" 1" 1"   6"   20"   1" 1½"

DRILLING PLAN FOR BALANCING STICKS

Plate D

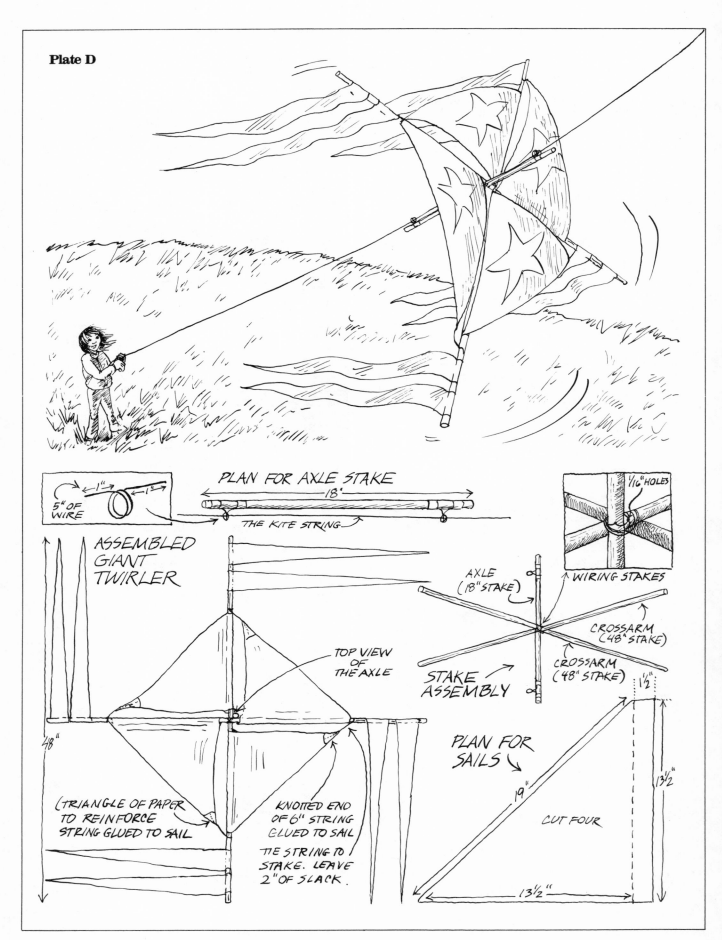

PLAN FOR AXLE STAKE

18'

THE KITE STRING

1" 1"

5" OF WIRE

1/16" HOLES

WIRING STAKES

ASSEMBLED GIANT TWIRLER

TOP VIEW OF THE AXLE

AXLE (18" STAKE)

CROSSARM (48" STAKE)

CROSSARM (48" STAKE)

STAKE ASSEMBLY

48"

(TRIANGLE OF PAPER TO REINFORCE STRING GLUED TO SAIL

KNOTTED END OF 6" STRING GLUED TO SAIL

TIE STRING TO STAKE. LEAVE 2" OF SLACK.

PLAN FOR SAILS

CUT FOUR

1/2"

13 1/2"

19"

13 1/2"

GIANT TWIRLER KITE CLIMBER

The Giant Twirler is a spectacular sight to see whirling up a kite string, especially when it is made of very bright colors. It is lighter and more versatile than the Tightrope Walker and can be constructed in any size that suits your kite. A whole party of kitefliers, sending these freewheelers spinning up their kite strings, can produce a glorious daytime fireworks display.

Tools and Materials

Drill: with a 1/16-inch bit
Needle-nose pliers
Scissors
White glue
Paintbrush
Bamboo garden stakes: approximately 3/8-inch in diameter — one piece, 18 inches long; two pieces, 48 inches long
Wrapping paper: white, one piece, 15 inches by 30 inches
Crepe paper: either sheets to cut into pennants or precut streamers
String
Wire: 22-gauge
Paint: artist's acrylics or oil
Adhesive tape

To Build a Giant Twirler

To make the frame, drill a 1/16-inch hole at the midpoint of each stake. Fasten the two 48-inch stakes together to form a cross with wire wound around and through the holes. Wire the 18-inch stake at its midpoint to the intersection of the cross but at right angles to the other stakes. (See the illustration, Plate D.) This forms the axle for the cross to spin on. The entire frame should be as rigid as possible.

Cut four wrapping paper sails to the dimensions given in the plans and decorate them with bright colors and bold designs. When the

paint is dry, fold the paper flaps along the broken lines, run a line of glue along the outside edge of the flaps, and glue a sail to each arm of the cross, as shown in the plan. Glue the knotted end of a six-inch length of string to the free corner of each sail and reinforce it with a triangle of paper glued on top. Tie the other end of each string to the nearest crossarm, leaving about 2 inches of slack between sail and crossarm.

To make the guide loops for the kite string, cut two 5-inch lengths of wire. Make a coil of each by wrapping the wire tightly and evenly around a pencil, leaving 1 inch of straight wire at each end. Bend these ends so that they are at right angles to the loops; then fasten them securely to the axle with adhesive tape, as shown. The two coils must be lined up exactly so that the kite string runs freely through them and is held clear of the frame.

Glue pennants or streamers to the ends of the crossarms. You will want to experiment with different sizes and lengths, but remember that they must all be the same weight, or the twirler will not balance correctly.

SAILBOAT KITE CLIMBER

Here is a kite climber that expands the fun and action. It not only sails up the string but comes back down again and will make as many sky voyages as you wish. This one has a simple single sail, but you could make a square-rigger with three or four masts using the same mechanism. Several boats on several strings can have exciting races and form a colorful regatta in the clouds.

Tools and Materials

Razor knife
Coping saw
Tin snips
Scissors
Needle-nose pliers
Hammer
Needle
Carpet thread and regular sewing thread
Balsa wood: one piece, 3/16 inch by 3 inches by 10 inches
Doweling: two pieces of 1/8-inch diameter, 10 inches long; two pieces of 1/2-inch diameter, 1/4 inch long
Wire: 18 inches of 18-gauge, 10 inches of 22-gauge
Cardboard: thin but stiff, one piece, 4 inches by 4 inches

Aluminum: 3/8 inch by 3 1/2 inches, two pieces cut from a can
Fabric: one piece of thin white cotton, 8 1/2 inches by 10 1/2 inches
Screw eye: one very small size
Metal ring: 1-inch curtain or keyring
Quarter-round molding: one piece, 1/4 inch by 15 inches long
Lead came: one piece, 4 inches long. This comes from stained-glass suppliers and is handy for ballast. The lead weights used for balancing tires will also work fine.
Staples: heavy 1/4-inch
Brads: 1/2-inch and 1-inch
Nail
White glue
Fine sandpaper
Paint: enamel or artist's acrylic

To Build a Sailboat Kite Climber

To make the boat, cut a hull shape from balsa wood and sand it well. For a mast, glue one flat edge of the piece of quarter round to the right, or starboard, side of the hull. It should be placed 1/2 inch from the bottom of the boat and 3 3/4 inches from the bow, or front, of the boat. Paint it as you desire. Fit a length of lead came over the edge of the hull bottom, and squeeze it in place.

To make the pulleys, cut four circles of cardboard from the pattern for pulley sides and mark the center points. Cut the two 1/4-inch slices of 1/2-inch doweling, sand them smooth, and mark the center points. Glue a cardboard circle to each side of the dowel slices, matching the centers. There must not be any cracks or gaps between the wood and cardboard for the kite string to catch in. Cut the pulley housings from an aluminum can and pierce the indicated holes. The small holes are made with a brad and the larger ones with a nail. Bend the housings along the broken lines, as shown in the pulley assembly diagram. Fit the pulley into the housing, matching the center points to the holes in the housing, and drive a 1-inch brad through housing and pulley. Center the pulley between the sides of the housing so that it will turn freely. Nail the pulleys at either end of the hull, as shown.

To make the sail release mechanism, cut a 12-inch length of 18-gauge wire; this will be the

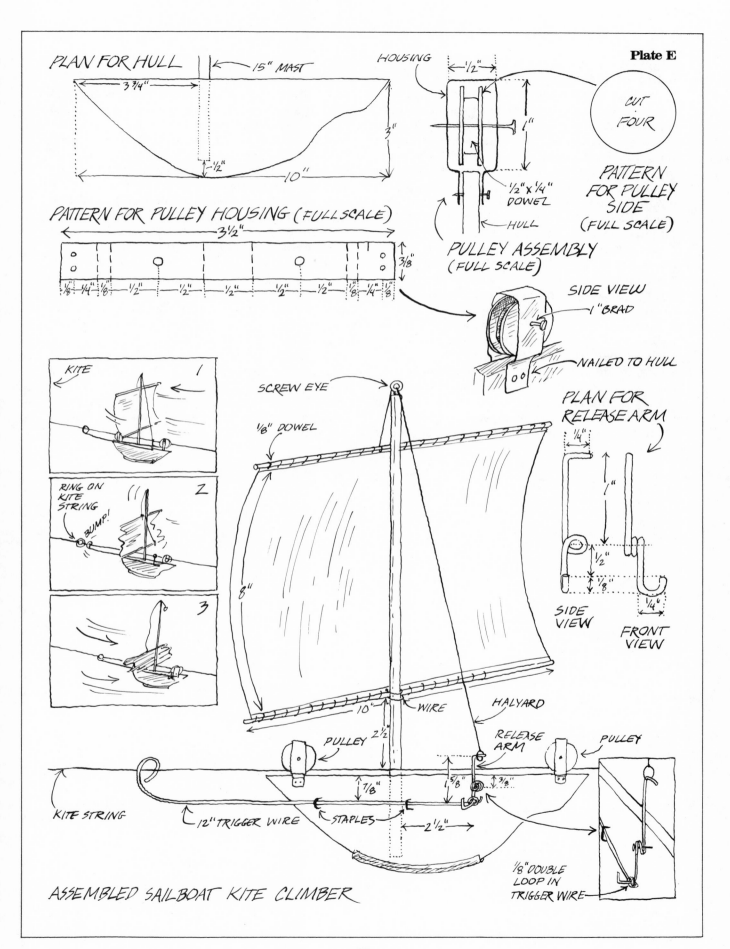

PLAN FOR HULL

3 3/4"

15" MAST

3"

1/2"

10"

HOUSING

1/2"

1"

1/2" x 1/4" DOWEL

HULL

Plate E

CUT FOUR

PATTERN FOR PULLEY SIDE (FULL SCALE)

PATTERN FOR PULLEY HOUSING (FULL SCALE)

3 1/2"

3/8"

1/8" 1/4" 1/8" 1/2" 1/2" 1/2" 1/2" 1/2" 1/8" 1/4" 1/8"

PULLEY ASSEMBLY (FULL SCALE)

SIDE VIEW

1" BRAD

NAILED TO HULL

KITE

1

RING ON KITE STRING

BUMP!

2

3

SCREW EYE

1/8" DOWEL

8"

10"

WIRE

2 1/2"

PULLEY

7/8"

KITE STRING

12" TRIGGER WIRE

STAPLES

HALYARD

RELEASE ARM

1 5/8"

3/8"

2 1/2"

PLAN FOR RELEASE ARM

1/4"

1"

1/2"

1/8"

1/4"

SIDE VIEW

FRONT VIEW

PULLEY

1/8" DOUBLE LOOP IN TRIGGER WIRE

ASSEMBLED SAILBOAT KITE CLIMBER

87

trigger wire. Bend it, as shown in the plan, with a 1/8-inch double loop at one end — made by wrapping the wire twice around a large nail — and a one-inch single loop at the other end. Cut a 2 1/2-inch length of 18-gauge wire for the release arm, and bend it to the shape shown in the plan. Fasten the release wire to the port, or left, side of the hull with a small brad through the center coil. This should be 3/8 inch below the deck line and 2 1/2 inches behind the mast. Fasten the trigger wire to the hull with staples, parallel to and 7/8 inch below the deck, curving up in front of the bow so that the large single loop is in line with the pulleys. The 1/8-inch double loop at the end of the trigger wire is hooked to the lower end of the release arm.

To make the sail, turn under and sew a 1/4-inch hem along both of the 8-inch sides and, with carpet threads, lace them to 1/8-inch spars, made of doweling. Fix the screw eye at the top of the mast. Fasten the lower spar tightly to the front of the mast with 22-gauge wire about 2 1/2 inches above the deck. Tie a 15-inch length of carpet thread to the center of the top spar; run the loose end through the screw eye at the top of the mast to serve as a halyard. Make a ring of 22-gauge wire, 3/16 inch in diameter. Tie this ring to the loose end of the halyard at the point where it will just hook over the top of the upright release arm with the sail fully hoisted. Test the mechanism by gently pushing on the front loop of the trigger wire; the release arm should pull forward out of the ring and release the halyard so that the sail drops. You may have to adjust the tension on the halyard or bend the wires slightly to make it operate smoothly.

To provide a stop that will activate the trigger wire, you must tie a 1-inch metal ring to the kite string at a point several feet below the kite. Before sending the sailboat up the string, test it, as you did the Tightrope Walker, to make sure that it does not "turn turtle." Thread a string through the pulleys and the ring in the trigger wire and hang it like a clothesline. If the boat capsizes, you will need to add more lead to the keel. When the boat balances nicely, it is ready for its maiden voyage.

SAIL CAR

This is a model of an old-fashioned western sail car just like the ones used in place of handcars to carry men and tools along the railroad tracks. These cars could not tack because they were confined to tracks. Some, however, were reported to reach speeds of forty miles per hour when running before the wind. As early as 1698, Sir Humphrey Mackworth used a sail car with success on a mining railway in South Wales. In 1807 a sail car on the Swansea and Mumbles Railway in Wales covered four and a half miles in forty-five minutes.

This model is designed to run on pavement. It is quite light, being made of balsa wood, so you will need to make several small sandbags to use as ballast. If two or more people make them, they are fun to race. The sailor who is most successful in adjusting his sails and ballast to the wind conditions will win.

Tools and Materials

Drill: with 1/8-inch, 1/4-inch, and 3/16-inch bits
Knife: paring or jackknife
Coping saw
Hacksaw
Drawing compass
Ruler
Needles: darning and light sewing
Sandpaper
Paintbrush
White glue
Brass tubing: 3/16-inch diameter, 5 inches

Nuts and bolts: two 1/8-inch bolts, 4 inches long, with nuts
Doweling: 1/4-inch diameter — one piece, 9 inches long; 1/16-inch diameter — one piece, 13 inches and one piece, 11 inches long
Balsa wood: one piece, 1 inch by 2 inches by 1/2 inch (axle supports); one piece, 2 inches by 6 inches by 1/4 inch (floor); two pieces, 3 inches by 6 inches by 1/4 inch (wheels); two pieces, 1 1/2 inches by 6 inches by 1/8 inch (body sides); and three pieces, 1/4 inch by 6 inches by 1/8 inch (side trim, cleats, and railings); hobby stores often have pre-packaged bags of assorted sizes
Tracing paper
Fabric: a 10- by 24-inch piece of white cotton
Thread: white carpet and button thread, regular white sewing thread
Screw eye: brass, one small
Primer sealer
Paint: artist's acrylic or model
Wire: 18-gauge

To Build a Sail Car

To make the body of the car, cut four axle supports from balsa wood (Plate F), and drill 1/4-inch holes through them. Cut, sand, and glue together the floor and sides of the cart, following the plan. Cut and shape the four trim pieces. Sand and glue them in place. Cut and glue the two 6-inch top railings. Carve two small cleats, and glue one to the center of the right-hand railing and the other to the center rear edge of the floor, as shown.

To step or put in the mast (Plate F), cut a 9-inch length of 1/4-inch doweling. Sand one end until it is slightly tapered toward the top, but not too small to hold the screw eye without splitting. Put in the screw eye carefully, where shown. Drill a 1/4-inch hole in the exact center of the floor and glue the mast into this hole.

With the hacksaw, cut two 2 1/2-inch pieces of the brass tubing. File the cut ends smooth. Insert the tubing through the holes in the axle supports; then glue the supports to the bottom of the car, as shown. Make sure that the tubing is parallel to the ends of the car.

To make the wheels (Plate F), draw four 2 1/2-inch circles with the compass on the 3- by 6- by 1/4-inch pieces of balsa wood and cut

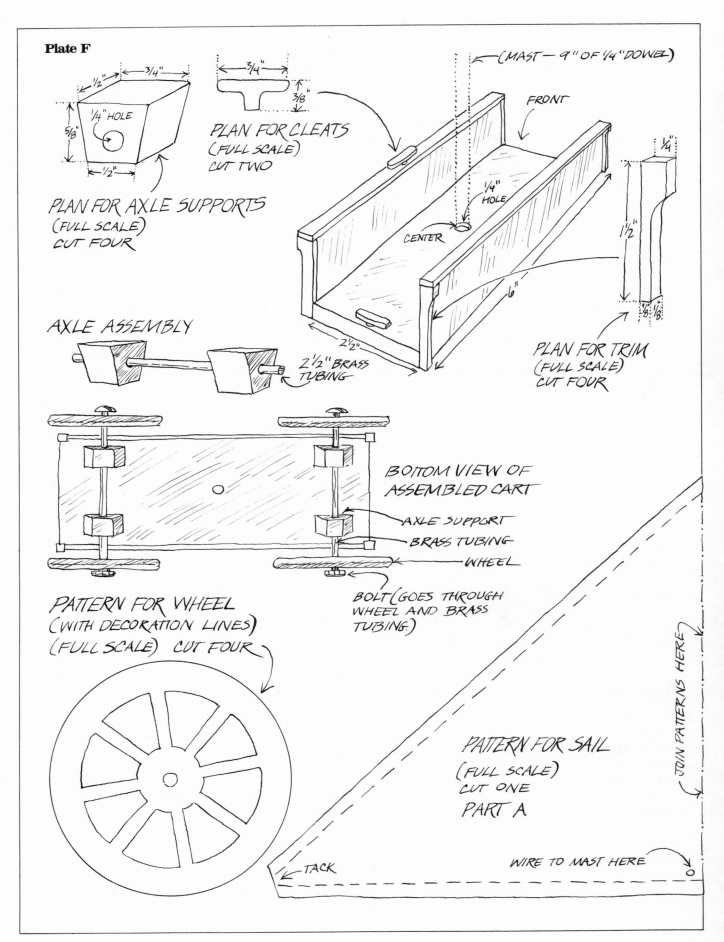

Plate F

(MAST — 9" OF ¼" DOWEL)

¼" HOLE

½" · ¾"

5/8"

½"

PLAN FOR AXLE SUPPORTS
(FULL SCALE)
CUT FOUR

¾"

3/8"

PLAN FOR CLEATS
(FULL SCALE)
CUT TWO

FRONT

¼" HOLE

CENTER

6"

2½"

¼"

1½"

1/8" 1/8"

PLAN FOR TRIM
(FULL SCALE)
CUT FOUR

AXLE ASSEMBLY

2½" BRASS TUBING

BOTTOM VIEW OF ASSEMBLED CART

AXLE SUPPORT

BRASS TUBING

WHEEL

BOLT (GOES THROUGH WHEEL AND BRASS TUBING.)

PATTERN FOR WHEEL
(WITH DECORATION LINES)
(FULL SCALE) CUT FOUR

PATTERN FOR SAIL
(FULL SCALE)
CUT ONE
PART A

JOIN PATTERNS HERE

TACK

WIRE TO MAST HERE

90

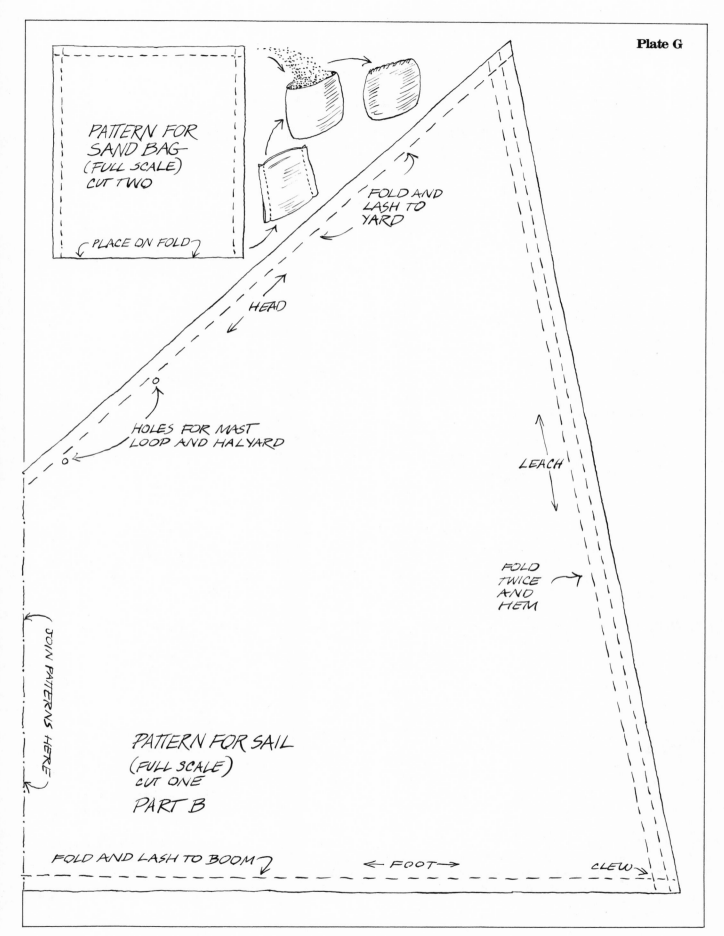

PATTERN FOR
SAND BAG
(FULL SCALE)
CUT TWO

PLACE ON FOLD

FOLD AND
LASH TO
YARD

HEAD

HOLES FOR MAST
LOOP AND HALYARD

LEACH

FOLD
TWICE
AND
HEM

JOIN PATTERNS HERE

PATTERN FOR SAIL
(FULL SCALE)
CUT ONE
PART B

FOLD AND LASH TO BOOM

← FOOT →

CLEW

Plate G

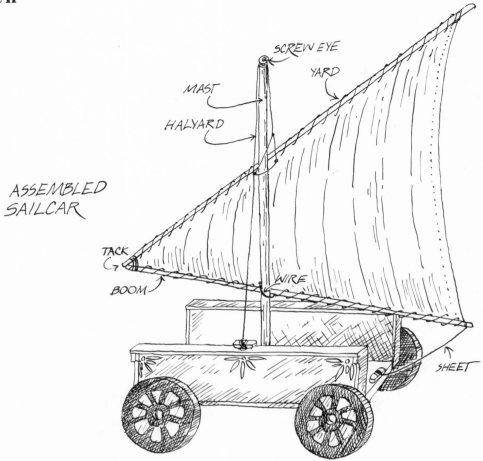

them out carefully, using a coping saw. Sand the edges until they are very smooth and round. Drill a 1/8-inch hole in the center of each wheel. Give the wheels and car a coat of primer sealer.

To make the sail (Plates F and G), cut a 13-inch yard and an 11-inch boom from the 1/16-inch doweling. Trace the sail pattern on tracing paper, joining the two parts of the pattern where indicated. Pin the pattern you've made onto the fabric and cut out. On the sails, draw in the lines shown with a pencil on both sides. These would be seam lines on a full-size sail. Hem the leach with regular sewing thread. Fold the head and foot of the sail along broken lines and, with carpet thread and darning needle, lace them to the spars. Spar is the general term for masts, booms, and yards. Leave about 12 inches of thread at the bottom corner, or clew, to act as a sheet. Sew a loop of thread, as shown, along the yard and leave a length of thread about 18 inches long, to raise and lower the sail. Bind the spars together tightly with thread at the tack.

To complete the sail car, resand the car and wheels, then paint. The car body is traditionally a dull, brick red with black trim and bright yellow fancy work. The wheels are usually white with black spokes and rims. When the paint is dry, attach the wheels with bolts through the axle tubes. Put on the nuts; then saw off any excess bolt with the hacksaw. Rig the sail by slipping the loop of thread at the head of the sail over the top of the mast. Insert a 1 1/2-inch wire through the sail where indicated; take it around the boom and then around the mast, about 1 3/4 inches from the bottom. Twist the wire tightly so the boom won't slide up or down the mast. Thread the halyard through the screw eye, hoist the sail, and tie it to the cleat on the railing. The cleat at the back of the car is for adjusting the mainsheet. Use the thread left hanging at the clew for this.

Cut four pieces of cotton the size of the sandbag pattern. Sew up the two long sides with small stitches. Then turn the bags inside out. Fill them with sand and stitch them closed.

PAPER YACHT

Have you ever felt like building a model sailboat and then decided that all of the wood carving involved would be just too much trouble? Future naval architects take notice; you can easily build this jumbo model of a gaff-rigged sloop without carving a sliver. She measures 36 inches from the tip of her bowsprit to the end of her boom and, although made entirely of cardboard and paper, she is constructed in much the same way as a real sailboat. This model is much too large for the bathtub, so you'll need to sail it in a fairly big pond. Once you have discovered how simple it is to build a cardboard boat, you can go on to design your own America's Cup contender.

Tools and Materials

Razor knife
Scissors
Ruler
Protractor
Paintbrush: small
Hammer
Needle-nose pliers
Darning needle
Carpet thread

Heavyweight cardboard: one piece, 30 inches by 3 inches; one piece, 30 inches by 6 inches; one piece, 14 inches by 5 inches; and small scraps for rigging
Lightweight cardboard: one piece, 8 inches by 12 inches and small scraps for rigging
Gummed brown wrapping tape: one roll, 2 inches wide
Newspapers: several days' worth, but only one if it's the Sunday *New York Times*
Fabric: lightweight cotton—one piece, 3 feet by 3 feet
Corks: two 1/2-inch
White glue
Masking tape
Sandpaper: fine
Tracing paper
Cotton cord
Wire, 18-gauge
Sand: fine
Paint, primer sealer and oil-base enamel

To Build a Paper Yacht

To make the mast and spars, roll moistened gummed tape into long tubes tapered at one end, as shown in the illustration. You will need to make the following: *Mainmast:* 23 inches long, 3/4 inch wide at the base, 1/2 inch at the tip. *Boom:* 22 inches long, 3/4 inch at the base, 1/2 inch at the tip. *Gaff:* 16 inches long, 1/2 inch at the base, a point at the tip. *Bowsprit:* 7 inches long, 5/8 inch at the base, a point at the tip. Let the spars dry thoroughly and trim them square at the ends.

To make the deck (Plate I), draw a center pencil line down the length of the 30- by 6-inch piece of cardboard. Draw lines intersecting the center line at right angles every 3 inches and measure to the left and right the distances shown on the deck plan. Draw a smooth curved line connecting these points and cut out the deck shape with sharp scissors or a razor knife. Cut a hole 1 inch in diameter on the center line, 10 inches from the bow. This will be for the mast.

To make the centerpiece (Plate I), mark the 30- by 3-inch piece of cardboard off into 3-inch sections. Mark off the measurements given in the centerpiece plan and cut out the shape. On the 14- by 5-inch piece of cardboard, draw and cut out the keel, taking

Plate I

MAKE THE SPARS (MAST, BOOM, GAFF, AND BOWSPRIT)
BY ROLLING GUMMED TAPE TO SIZES SPECIFIED IN TEXT.

TRIM SQUARE AT ENDS

PLAN FOR DECK

BOW

$1\frac{1}{8}"$ $1\frac{7}{8}"$ $2\frac{1}{2}"$ $2\frac{7}{8}"$ $3\frac{1}{8}"$ $3"$ $2\frac{5}{8}"$ $2\frac{1}{4}"$ $1\frac{5}{8}"$ STERN $\frac{1}{4}"$

$3"$ $3"$ $3"$ $3"$ $3"$ $3"$ $3"$ $3"$ $3"$ $3"$

PLAN FOR CENTERPIECE AND KEEL

$10"$ $13"$ $7"$

$3\frac{1}{2}"$

$1\frac{1}{8}"$ $2"$ $2\frac{1}{2}"$ $2\frac{7}{8}"$ $3"$ $2\frac{7}{8}"$ $2\frac{1}{2}"$ $2"$ $1\frac{1}{8}"$

$3"$ $3"$ $3"$ $3"$ $3"$ $3"$ $3"$ $3"$ $3"$ $3"$

PLAN FOR RIB ASSEMBLY

SECTION VIEW
SHOWING
CURVE OF
RIBS

(KEEL)

RIB

CENTER-
PIECE

DECK

TAPE CENTERPIECE TO DECK

$\frac{1}{2}"$ STRIPS OF
CARDBOARD

$2\frac{1}{4}"$ $3\frac{1}{4}"$ $4"$ $4\frac{1}{2}"$ $4\frac{5}{8}"$ $4\frac{3}{8}"$ $3\frac{7}{8}"$ $3\frac{1}{4}"$ $2"$

94

care that the top curve of the keel matches the bottom curve of the centerpiece and that the shape is similar to the one in the plan.

Place the deck flat on a tabletop with the marked center line showing. Then place the straight edge of the centerpiece along this line in an upright position. Fix it firmly in place with short strips of tape on either side. Cut lightweight cardboard info 1/2-inch strips and cut the strips into lengths twice as long as the measurement given in the rib plans, marking the center point as you go. Glue the center point of each rib to the edge of the centerpiece at the marked 3-inch intervals. Curve the ribs down and tape them to the edge of the deck to form a smooth, rounded hull shape. If you want to make an especially fine hull, glue additional ribs between these.

To sheath the hull (Plate J), cut newspapers into strips 3/4 inch wide by about 30 inches long. Paint them with slightly watered white glue and apply them one at a time down the length of the hull, across the ribs. Overlap the strips about 1/2 inch as you go. Keep the shape as smooth as possible and do not allow the paper to sag between the ribs. Let the hull dry thoroughly.

Cut more newspaper into 1-inch by 12-inch strips. Brush liberally with glue and lay them on one at a time sideways across the bottom of the hull and up and over the edge of the deck, so these strips will be going at right angles to the others you put on. Each strip should overlap the last by about 1/2 inch. You will need to apply seven or eight layers of newspaper, letting the hull dry between layers. Make each layer as smooth as you can and patch any dents or uneven spots with additional paper before adding the next layer.

When the last layer is dry (Plate J), tape the keel upright along the center line of the boat bottom, the long pointed end toward the bow, or front, and directly under the mast hole. Use overlapping strips of glued newspaper to cover the keel completely and attach it firmly to the hull. Fill the place where the keel meets the hull with additional strips of paper to form a smooth curve, as shown. Brush a final coat of unthinned glue over the keel and hull and let it dry completely. If you wish to refine the hull shape even more, you may give it a coat of premixed patching plaster; then sand the hull smooth when dry. Paint the hull bottom (not the deck) with primer sealer and finish it with at least two coats of enamel.

To finish the deck (Plate J) trace the pattern for the mast collar on lightweight cardboard and cut out. Roll it into a cylinder with ends just meeting and tape it, as illustrated. Center the collar over the mast hole and fasten it in place with small strips of glued newspaper. Trace the pattern for the bowsprit strap and cut it out of lightweight cardboard.

Fold along the broken lines, as shown in the plan. Stuff the open end of the rolled bowsprit to a depth of 1 inch with glued paper and glue it to the deck leaving 5 inches protruding beyond the bow. Fit the bowsprit strap over the base of the bowsprit and fasten the tabs to the deck with strips of glued newspaper.

Make three cleats of 18-gauge wire, following the plans. Fasten them to the deck, where shown, with several layers of newspaper. It is important that they be solidly fixed, so take special care with them.

To step or mount the mast (Plate J), make a 3-inch cut up both sides of the mast at the base. Apply glue to the end of the mast, inside and out, and insert the mast into the mast hole so that each side of the cut portion straddles the centerpiece. Cover the points where the deck, mast collar, and mast join with strips of glued paper.

In order to finish the deck, apply two very neat, smooth layers of newspaper strips carefully trimmed along the edge. When it is completely dry, cut two 1/2-inch holes in the deck, called "ballast holes" in the plan.

The next step will be to rig your boat (Plate K). Bend 18-gauge wire to form both the boom gooseneck and the gaff gooseneck, as shown in the plans. Make tight rolls of glued newspaper to hold the prongs of the goosenecks and insert them into the open ends of the rolled boom and gaff. Notice from the drawing that the gaff end must be formed into a sharp angle in order to attach to the mast properly. When they are dry, slip the boom and gaff onto the mast. Cut the crosstree from heavy cardboard following the pattern. The large hole should be sized to fit no more than 4 inches down from the top of the mast. Glue a strip of tape around the mast to prevent it slipping any farther down. Place the base of the topmast on the crosstree in front of the mainmast. Tape the two masts together. Glue a line of cotton cord all the way around the outside edge at the juncture of the sides and deck, as a toe rail. Paint the deck, masts, and spars with a coat of primer sealer and two coats of enamel.

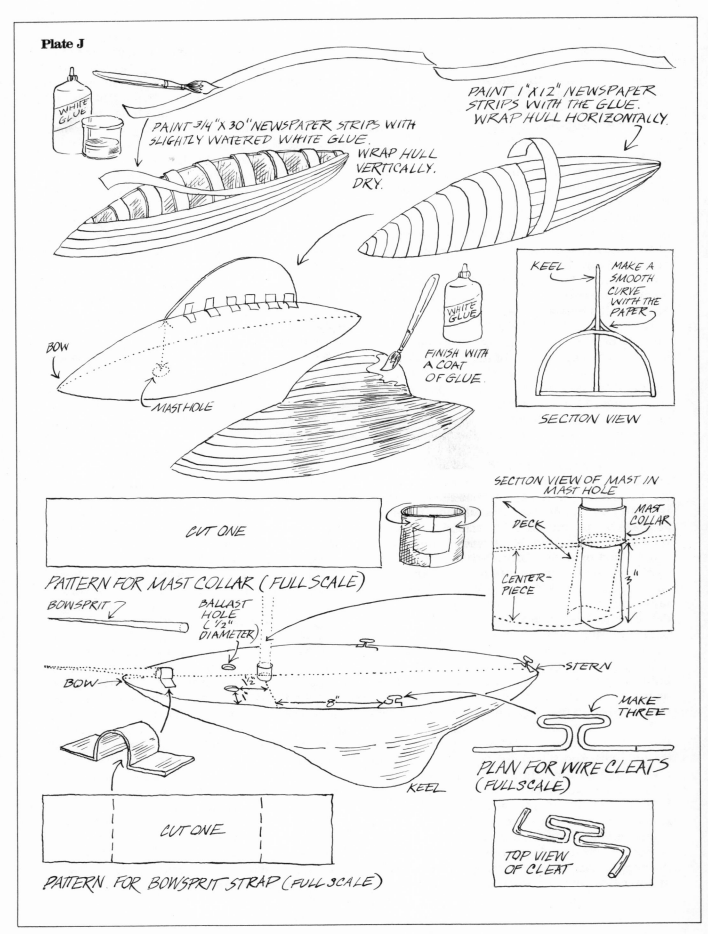

PAINT 3/4"X 30" NEWSPAPER STRIPS WITH SLIGHTLY WATERED WHITE GLUE.

WRAP HULL VERTICALLY. DRY.

PAINT 1"X 12" NEWSPAPER STRIPS WITH THE GLUE. WRAP HULL HORIZONTALLY.

WHITE GLUE

BOW

MAST HOLE

FINISH WITH A COAT OF GLUE.

WHITE GLUE

KEEL

MAKE A SMOOTH CURVE WITH THE PAPER

SECTION VIEW

CUT ONE

PATTERN FOR MAST COLLAR (FULL SCALE)

SECTION VIEW OF MAST IN MAST HOLE

DECK

MAST COLLAR

CENTER-PIECE

3"

BOWSPRIT

BALLAST HOLE (1/2" DIAMETER)

BOW

1/2"
1"

8"

STERN

MAKE THREE

KEEL

PLAN FOR WIRE CLEATS (FULL SCALE)

CUT ONE

PATTERN FOR BOWSPRIT STRAP (FULL SCALE)

TOP VIEW OF CLEAT

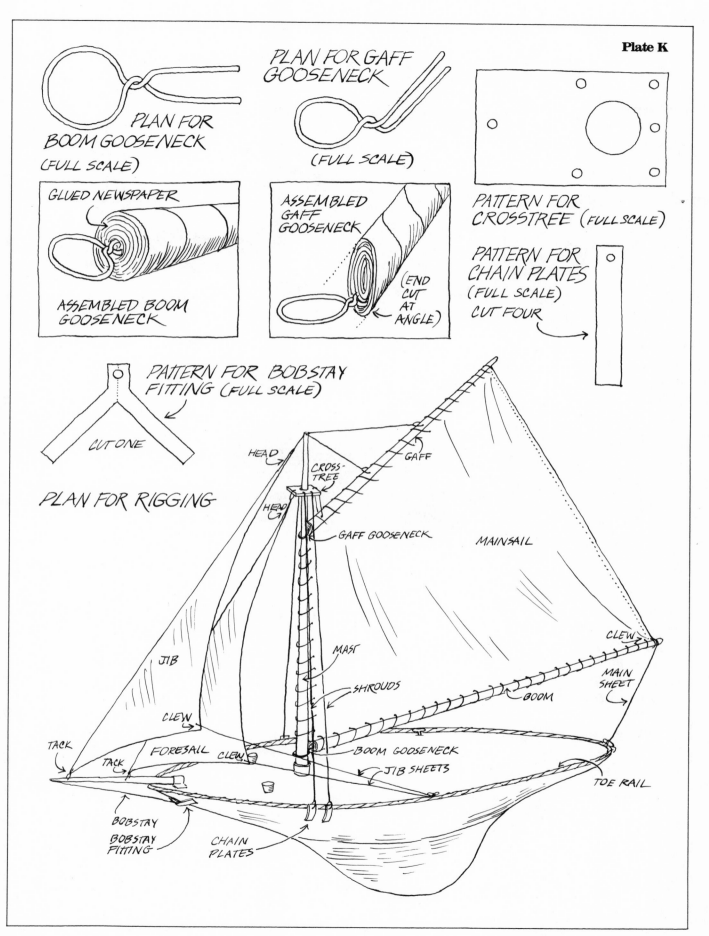

PLAN FOR
BOOM GOOSENECK
(FULL SCALE)

PLAN FOR GAFF
GOOSENECK
(FULL SCALE)

GLUED NEWSPAPER

ASSEMBLED BOOM
GOOSENECK

ASSEMBLED
GAFF
GOOSENECK

(END
CUT
AT
ANGLE)

PATTERN FOR
CROSSTREE (FULL SCALE)

PATTERN FOR
CHAIN PLATES
(FULL SCALE)
CUT FOUR

PATTERN FOR BOBSTAY
FITTING (FULL SCALE)

CUT ONE

PLAN FOR RIGGING

HEAD

CROSS-
TREE

GAFF

HEAD

GAFF GOOSENECK

MAINSAIL

MAST

SHROUDS

JIB

CLEW

CLEW

TACK

FORESAIL

CLEW

TACK

BOOM GOOSENECK

JIB SHEETS

CLEW

BOOM

MAIN
SHEET

TOE RAIL

BOBSTAY

BOBSTAY
FITTING

CHAIN
PLATES

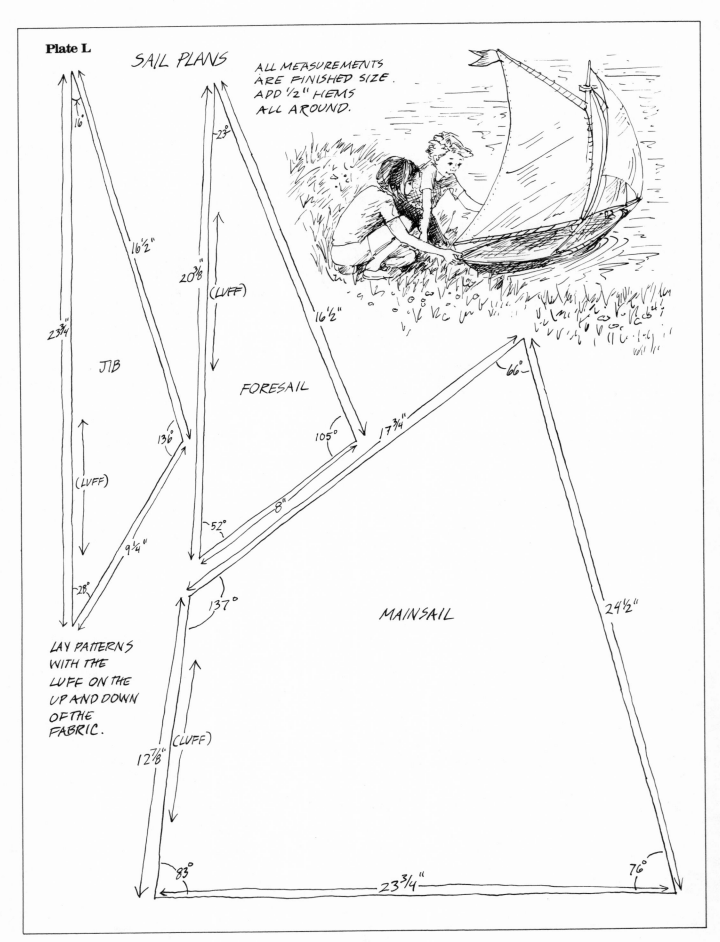

Plate L

SAIL PLANS

ALL MEASUREMENTS
ARE FINISHED SIZE.
ADD ½" HEMS
ALL AROUND.

16°

16½"

23¾"

JIB

(LUFF)

136°

9¼"

28°

LAY PATTERNS
WITH THE
LUFF ON THE
UP AND DOWN
OF THE
FABRIC.

23°

20⅜"

(LUFF)

16½"

105°

8"

52°

FORESAIL

137°

12⅞"

(CLUFF)

83°

17¾"

66°

24½"

MAINSAIL

23¾"

76°

Cut four chain plates and one bobstay fitting (Plate K) of heavy cardboard. Make the holes in them with a slender nail or darning needle. Give each of them two coats of black paint. Fold the bobstay fitting and glue it to the hull 3 inches below the bowsprit. Glue the chain plates to either side, one 10 inches from the bow and one 11 1/2 inches, as shown in the rigging plans. Using carpet thread, tie the shrouds to the holes in the chain plates and the holes in the crosstree. Sew a 12-inch thread through the tip of the bowsprit and tie it. Take the other end through the hole in the bobstay fitting, pull it taut, and tie.

To make the sails (Plate L), cut the fabric to the sizes and shapes shown, remembering that you must add 1/2 inch all the way around for hems. The luff of the sails should be straight up and down on the fabric. Turn and sew the hems. Sew 18-inch lengths of carpet thread to the clews of the jib and foresail for sheets. Sew 4-inch lengths of thread to the heads and tacks of both sails. Run the headline of the foresail through the front hole in the crosstree and tie it. Sew the tackline of the foresail through the bowsprit 4 1/2 inches in from the tip and tie it. Attach the jib by sewing the headline through the tip of the mast and tying it. Sew the tackline through the bowsprit 1 1/2 inches from the tip and tie it. The jib and foresail lines act as stays to hold the mast in an upright position and should be just long enough to be taut with-out pulling the mast forward. Lace the mainsail to the mast, boom, and gaff so that the hems are held close to but not over the spars. Tie a 20-inch mainsheet to the end of the boom.

Sew a 20-inch length of line through the top of the mast and tie it, leaving an even amount of thread on either side. Sew one end of the thread through the gaff about 7 inches from the end of the gaff. Don't knot it though. Sew the other end through the gaff 5 inches from the gooseneck and leave it loose too. Now pull these threads; tighten the gaff up until the mainsail is almost flat and tie a knot in each to hold the mainsail taut. Sew a short length of thread through the gaff close to the gooseneck and tie this thread through the rear hole in the crosstree to keep the gooseneck from slipping down the mast.

Before putting the boat in the water, you must give it some ballast, or weight, to hold it upright and steady. Pour sand into the hull through the two holes in the deck, taking care that you put the same amount on each side of the centerpiece. When the yacht rides in the water so that its deck is about an inch above the water, close the ballast holes with corks, and you are ready to sail. Your paper yacht will be quite watertight and seaworthy if you have painted it with care. The yacht will last for a long time if you are careful to store it in a dry place *with the ballast corks removed* when you are not using it.

PART FIVE

RUBBER BAND POWERED TOYS

There's Something of a Twist in This

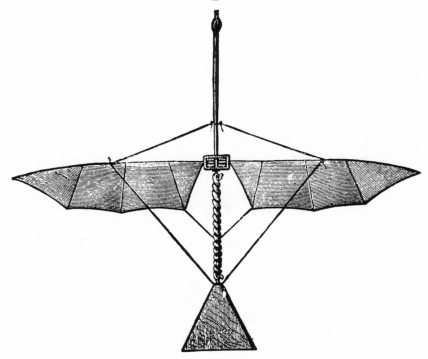

Nobody knows who first discovered rubber, but it was used by South American Indians as early as 1493. Christopher Columbus reported seeing the natives playing a game with a ball made of a gumlike substance that bounced. By 1736 when the French explorer Charles de la Condamine brought samples of this strange material back to Europe, the Amazonian Indians were making a number of articles with it. They had learned to make boots by repeatedly dipping their feet into latex. They could waterproof cloth, and they made bottles by coating a clay mold with many layers of latex. When the latex dried, they broke the mold and extracted the clay. We were delighted to read of another Indian invention, the squirt gun! They put reed nozzles on hollow balls that were then filled with water and squirted at each other during celebrations.

In 1770 an English scientist discovered that a piece of hardened latex would erase pencil marks if rubbed hard enough on the paper, hence the name "rubber." By the end of the century, a brisk trade in rubber boots and bottles had developed between South America and Europe. Rubber bands, so the story goes, were invented in the 1830s by another Englishman who simply sliced up a rubber bottle into rings. At that moment a whole new era in toymaking was inaugurated.

One of the first toys to make use of this new form for rubber was the catapult, a much more efficient version of the old-fashioned sling. As one 1890s source states, "Catapults may be used by skilled shooters with almost as much effect as fire-arms, and they are nearly as dangerous, not to the shooter, but to other people." Catapults were soon forbidden in London and other large cities, but they remained a cherished possession of country boys. Our paper cannon is a glorified and benevolent version of the catapult and a happy reprieve for small birds and barn cats.

Another toymaking device that soon developed was the use of a twisted rubber band to power boats. These craft ranged from elaborate models with screw propellers to flat boards with paddle wheels. A similar motor runs our Unicycle Race and can be adapted to a variety of uses with only minor changes. The upright axle can be lengthened to make an airplane merry-go-round or shortened to turn a carousel.

While the Unicycle Race will require three hours or more to build, our little String Climbers can be cut and assembled in about an hour, once you get the hang of them. We have no idea where or when they originated, but our monkey is very much like one shown in an 1896 children's magazine.

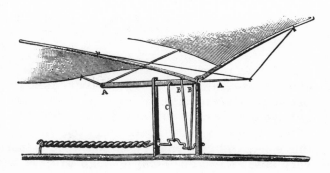

The fly-fly employs the most imaginative use of rubber band power. It wasn't designed as a toy at all, but rather as a serious experiment in artificial flight. Alphonse Penaud, a pioneer in the field, developed these models in the 1870s, thirty years before the first manned flights. In this version, the wings flapped like a bird's.

A trolley car and a bicycle race made of cardboard and powered by rubber bands.

A second and more successful fly-fly used a rubber band to drive a propeller. Penaud's biggest contribution was the development of the automatic rudder, the small wings placed behind the main wings.

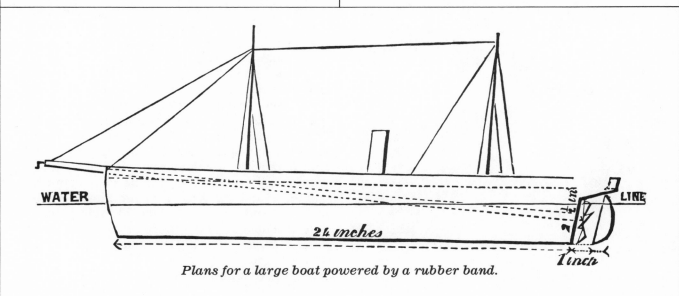

Plans for a large boat powered by a rubber band.

MONKEY ON A STRING

These whimsical toys are familiar to many of us. They climb up a string in a very lifelike manner. The fascinating thing is that you really have to look hard to see what makes them climb. You can make them from any strong thin wood. Old-fashioned cigar box wood is the very best, if you are lucky enough to have a supply that you don't mind using. They can also be made from heavy cardboard, but won't be as handsome or durable.

Tools and Materials

Coping saw
Drill: with 5/64-inch bit
Paintbrush
Wood rasp
Needle-nose pliers
Knife: paring or jackknife
Vise
Clamp: small size
Plywood: 1/8-inch (or heavy cardboard)
Wire: 18-gauge
White glue
Rubber band: lightweight, 1 1/2 inches long
Round toothpick
Paints: artist's acrylic or oil
String: strong and light or button thread
Tracing paper
Sandpaper

To Build a Monkey

Trace the patterns of the Monkey's body, arms, and legs separately, and cut them out of paper. Lay the patterns on the wood (or cardboard) and outline them; cut two legs, two arms, and one body. Hold the two legs together in a vise to finish the edges, first with a wood rasp, then with sandpaper, until the pieces match exactly. Do the same with the two arms. Finish and sand the body edges.

Hold the two arms together with a clamp and drill a hole through the hands. Drill four holes in the legs, as shown in the patterns, in the same manner. Make sure the holes match exactly. Drill the hole in the body at the hip. Glue the arms securely to the body in the position shown.

Using a knife, cut three 1/2-inch pieces from the center section of the round toothpick. Glue one piece of toothpick into each of the three lower holes in one leg. Put the rubber band around the toothpick in the toe, then glue on the second leg, matching up the toothpicks and the holes. Let the glue dry; then paint all of the pieces brown, if you are making the monkey. Make a tail of brown yarn, or felt, threaded on a light wire and curled up like a happy monkey's. Big goggly movable eyes will help make him funny. You can find packaged eyeballs of various sizes in many craft stores, but *be warned* — once you start glueing them onto things, you will find it hard to stop.

Attach the monkey's legs to the body with 18-gauge wire, just loose enough so they move freely. Wire the paws together at the top. Thread the 30-inch string between the heel and toe pegs, around the back of the knee peg, then up through the front of the paws, as shown. The paws should be wired so close together that the string will just pull through with some resistance. Bring the rubber band up between the arms and slip it over the monkey's head. This will pull the legs up into a sitting position. Hold the string above and below the monkey. Pull it taut, then slacken it, and the monkey will shinny up the string. If he doesn't move easily, adjust the tension of the paws. We've included patterns for other climbing characters, but don't stop there. You could do a panda, a gorilla, a koala, or a prince on his way to rescue a princess. How about a life-sized one to climb the side of a building?

Plate A

ARMS GLUED
TO BODY

HAND ASSEMBLY

WIRE HANDS
TOGETHER
THROUGH HOLES.

LEG ASSEMBLY

WIRE TOP OF LEG TO
BODY THROUGH HOLES.

GLUE TOOTHPICK
SECTIONS INTO
HOLES IN LEGS.

½" — ½" — ½"

ROUNDED TOOTHPICK
CUT INTO SECTIONS

METHOD OF
STRINGING CLIMBERS

STRING →

RUBBER
BAND

PATTERNS FOR CLIMBING FIGURES
(FULL SCALE)

PAINT ON
EYES OR
GLUE ON
MOVABLE
EYES

ARMS
CUT TWO

BODY
CUT ONE

LEGS
CUT TWO

TAIL
YARN GLUED
AROUND
WIRE

UNICYCLE RACE

Here are plans for a surprisingly efficient rubber-band motor that sends two clowns pedaling wildly around in a circle. You can make any kind of wheeled figures that you like for this motor, even small automobiles or trains, but the pedaling figures with jointed legs will produce the funniest action.

Tools and Materials

Needle-nose pliers
Scissors
Saw
Paintbrush: small
Razor knife
Drill: with 3/8-inch bit
Cardboard: mediumweight, very stiff, one piece, 11 inches by 18 inches and one piece, 3 inches by 5 inches
Paint: artist's acrylics
Wire: 18-gauge and 22-gauge
White glue

Beads: twenty, 1/8-inch round beads with holes large enough for 18-gauge wire to turn easily inside them
Box: a small, sturdy wood or cardboard box about 4 inches wide, 6 inches long, and 2 inches deep (you could make one)
Doweling: one piece of 1/4-inch diameter, 36 inches long
Brads: one, 1/2 inch long
Staples: one, 1/2 inch wide
Rubber bands
Tracing paper
Masking tape

To Build a Unicycle Race

To make the clowns (Plate B), trace their patterns and cut from stiff cardboard. Cut two bodies with right arms only and two with left arms only. Glue the right-arm bodies to the left-arm bodies above the glue line, leaving the lower bodies and center posts unglued. Cut

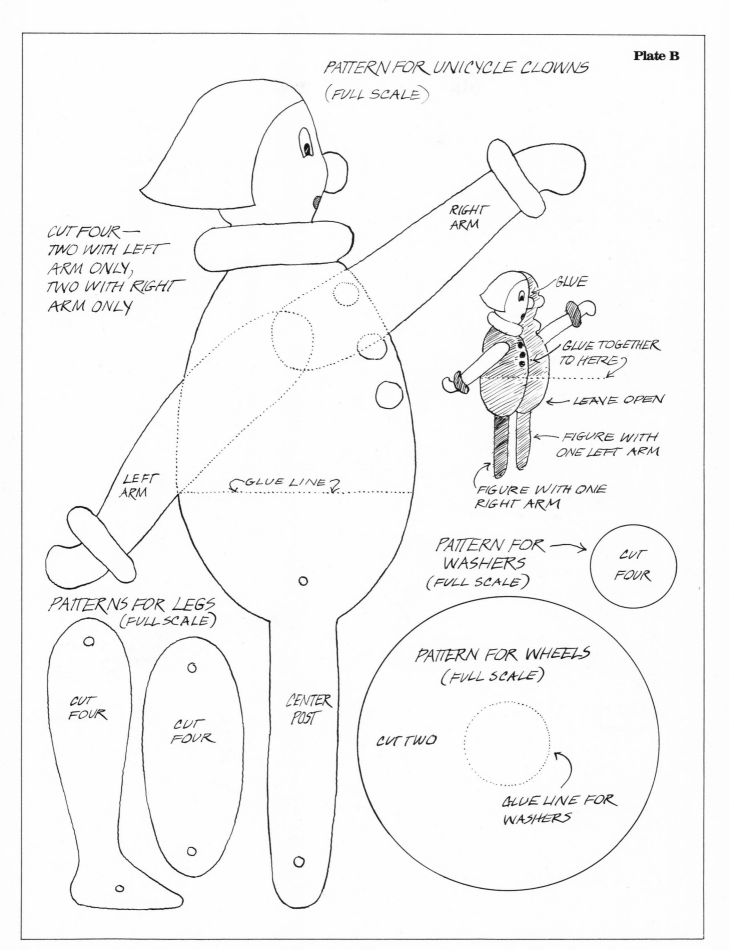

PATTERN FOR UNICYCLE CLOWNS
(FULL SCALE)

CUT FOUR—
TWO WITH LEFT
ARM ONLY,
TWO WITH RIGHT
ARM ONLY

RIGHT
ARM

GLUE

GLUE TOGETHER
TO HERE

LEAVE OPEN

FIGURE WITH
ONE LEFT ARM

LEFT
ARM

GLUE LINE

FIGURE WITH ONE
RIGHT ARM

PATTERN FOR
WASHERS
(FULL SCALE)

CUT
FOUR

PATTERNS FOR LEGS
(FULL SCALE)

CUT
FOUR

CUT
FOUR

CENTER
POST

PATTERN FOR WHEELS
(FULL SCALE)

CUT TWO

GLUE LINE FOR
WASHERS

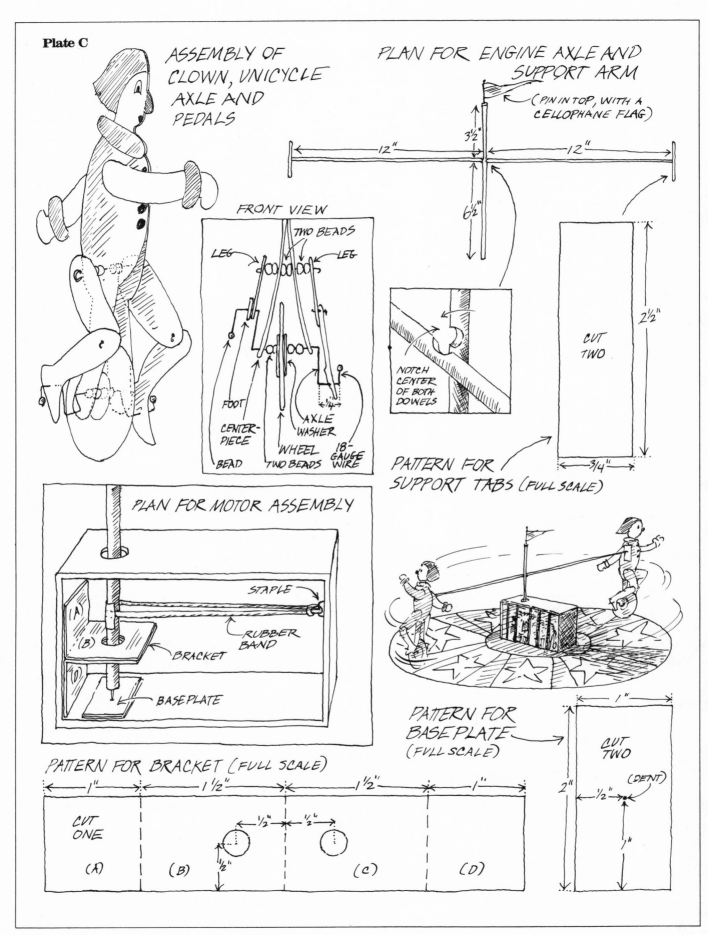

Plate C

ASSEMBLY OF CLOWN, UNICYCLE AXLE AND PEDALS

PLAN FOR ENGINE AXLE AND SUPPORT ARM

(PIN IN TOP, WITH A CELLOPHANE FLAG)

3½"

6½"

12"

12"

FRONT VIEW

TWO BEADS

LEG

LEG

FOOT

CENTER-PIECE

BEAD

WHEEL TWO BEADS

AXLE WASHER

18-GAUGE WIRE

¼"

NOTCH CENTER OF BOTH DOWELS

CUT TWO

2½"

¾"

PATTERN FOR SUPPORT TABS (FULL SCALE)

PLAN FOR MOTOR ASSEMBLY

STAPLE

RUBBER BAND

BRACKET

BASEPLATE

(A)

(B)

(D)

PATTERN FOR BASEPLATE (FULL SCALE)

1"

CUT TWO

2"

½"

(DENT)

1"

PATTERN FOR BRACKET (FULL SCALE)

1"

1½"

1½"

1"

CUT ONE

(A)

(B)

(C)

(D)

½"

½"

½"

two wheels and four washers from cardboard. Glue a washer on either side of the wheels, matching centers. Make holes where indicated in all of the pieces and paint them as you like. Remember that the center posts will be part of the unicycles and not part of the clowns, so paint them appropriately.

To assemble the figures (Plate C), attach the upper and lower leg pieces together by running a short piece of 22-gauge wire through the holes and making a loop on both sides. The joints should be loose enough to move easily. Attach the upper legs to the hole above the center post in the same manner, but insert two beads as spacers between each leg and body section and two beads between the halves of the body. Use the heavier, 18-gauge wire for this. Again the joints must be very loose so that the legs move freely.

To make the axle (Plate C), cut a 4-inch length of 18-gauge wire. Center a wheel on this. It should fit tight, so put a drop of glue on either side to hold the wheel in place. Follow the plan for assembling the axles. Put the beads and center posts on the wire before you bend the pedals. Then put on the feet and outside beads. Hold the clown upright and roll the wheel along a flat surface to make sure that all of the parts move easily.

To make the axle and support arms (Plate C), cut a 10-inch length of doweling. Drive the 1/2-inch brad about halfway into one end. Measure 6 1/2 inches up from the brad and cut a notch about 1/3 inch wide halfway into the

dowel. Cut a 24-inch length of doweling. Notch it in the same manner. Glue the two dowels together where each is notched at right angles to each other. Cut two cardboard support tabs and glue them onto the ends of the arm.

To make the motor (Plate C), drill a 3/8-inch hole in the top of the box, centered and 1 inch in from the inside wall of the box. Make and position the bracket directly under the hole so that the hole in the bracket and the hole in the box are in line. Cut two cardboard baseplates and glue them one on top of the other. Make a center hole just slightly larger than the head of the brad in the baseplates. Glue them both to the bottom of the box so that the axle is held perfectly vertical and spins freely. Fasten a long rubber band to a staple driven into the side of the box (if wood), or pull the rubber band through a hole in the side of the box (if cardboard), and knot it securely. Loop the other end of the rubber band around the axle dowel and tape it so that it winds onto the dowel when the axle turns. Paint and decorate the motor box and support arm as desired.

Glue the clowns to the support tabs so that the unicycle wheels just touch the ground. Wind the toy by turning the clowns backwards. Let go and they will chase each other around at a great rate. If your box is made of cardboard, you might have trouble with it tipping over. You can make the entire toy a lot more substantial if you mount it on a 26-inch circle of plywood, painted to look like a circus ring.

HOUSE ARTILLERY

Here is a working cannon that shoots Ping-Pong balls 20 feet or more. This is a great rainy day project, since it is made of materials you are apt to have around the house. It is relatively safe to shoot indoors. The Ping-Pong balls are too light to do damage, but don't aim the cannon at anything fragile — just the same.

Tools and Materials

Scissors
Saw
Drill: with 1/8-inch bit
Wire cutters
Razor knife
Drawing compass
Paintbrush: for glue
Heavy brown wrapping paper: two pieces, 30 inches by 48 inches
Brown gummed tape: 2 inches wide
Dowel: 1/4-inch diameter, 8 inches long
Spools: three wooden or plastic sewing-thread
Wire: 14-, 18- and 22-gauge
Cardboard: heavyweight
Cotter pins: six, 1 inch
Rubber bands: six heavy-duty, 1/4 inch by 3 1/2 inches
Adhesive tape or reinforced packing tape: 1/2 inch wide
Cord: strong cotton, 30 inches long
White glue

To Build a Cannon

Cover one side of a 30- by 48-inch sheet of wrapping paper with a generous coat of white glue and roll it into a tapered tube (Plate D). One end should measure about 3 inches in diameter, the other about 4 inches. It might be a good idea to roll the paper up to the right size once without glue, to get the feel of it. Spread glue on the second sheet of paper and roll it around the first tube for extra strength. Make the tube as straight and as perfectly round as you can. While it dries, go on to the next step.

To make the gun carriage (Plate D), cut four 8-inch circles of heavy cardboard and glue them together to make two double-thick wheels. Make a 3/8-inch hole in the center of each with the point of the scissors. Saw two spools in half and glue the halves to each side of the wheel centers to make hubs. Cut two strips of heavy cardboard to the dimensions shown in the carriage plan (Plate D). Glue the slanted ends together only as far as the dotted line shown. Let dry.

To make the shot thrower, cut two disks 3 inches in diameter from heavy cardboard and glue them together. Make a ring 2 inches in diameter and 1 inch high (like a napkin ring) from several layers of light cardboard strips. Glue this to the double cardboard disk, as shown. Make three evenly spaced holes around the disk, 1/4 inch from the edge. Bend a piece of 18-gauge wire into a circle 3 inches in diameter. Slip three rubber bands on it. This wire ring goes around the edge of the disk with a rubber band at each hole. Use a light wire twisted through each hole to hold a rubber band and the wire ring securely to the disk. Twist the other ends of the light wires together at the center back of the disk, as shown. Loop and secure a second rubber band through each of the others. Set the shot thrower aside until the glue is thoroughly dry.

When the gun barrel is dry, trim it at both ends to a 22-inch length. Cut two disks of cardboard to the exact circumference of the larger end. Glue the disks together and make a 1/4-inch hole in the center. Glue a half spool over the hole, matching the hole in the spool with the hole in the disk. Fasten the disk to the large end of the cannon barrel with gummed tape, the spool half on the outside. Mark a 2 1/2-inch diameter circle 4 inches from the large end of the barrel. Cut it carefully with a razor knife, leaving 1 inch uncut for a hinge. You may want to reinforce the hinge with adhesive tape. Bend a piece of 14-gauge wire into

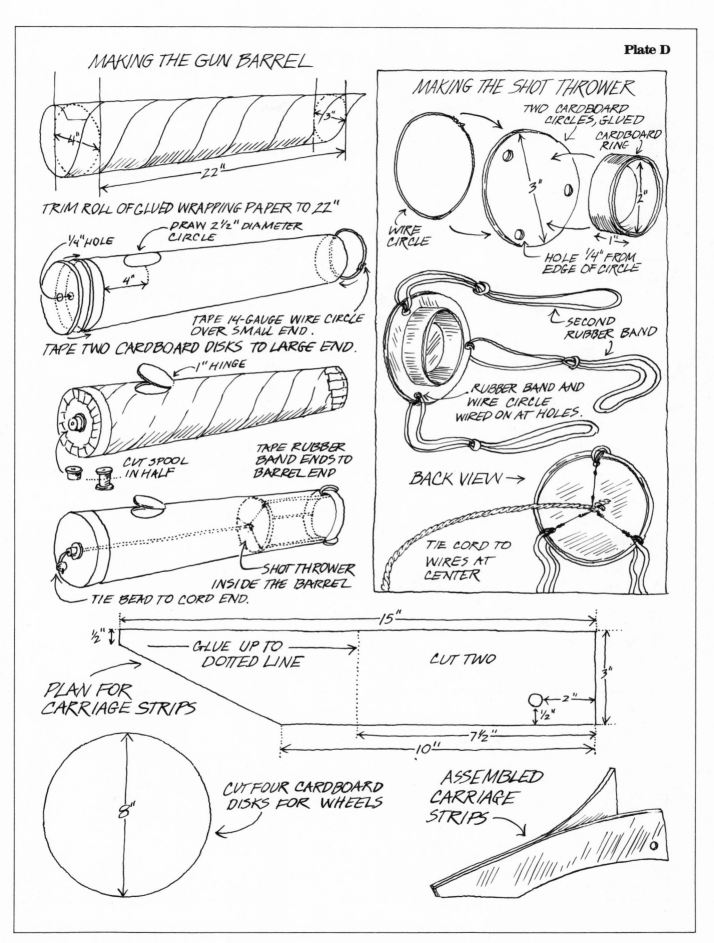

MAKING THE GUN BARREL

22"

4"

3"

TRIM ROLL OF GLUED WRAPPING PAPER TO 22"

1/4" HOLE

DRAW 2½" DIAMETER CIRCLE

4"

TAPE 14-GAUGE WIRE CIRCLE OVER SMALL END.

TAPE TWO CARDBOARD DISKS TO LARGE END.

1" HINGE

CUT SPOOL IN HALF

TAPE RUBBER BAND ENDS TO BARREL END

SHOT THROWER INSIDE THE BARREL

TIE BEAD TO CORD END.

Plate D

MAKING THE SHOT THROWER

TWO CARDBOARD CIRCLES, GLUED

CARDBOARD RING

3"

2"

1"

WIRE CIRCLE

HOLE 1/4" FROM EDGE OF CIRCLE

SECOND RUBBER BAND

RUBBER BAND AND WIRE CIRCLE WIRED ON AT HOLES.

BACK VIEW →

TIE CORD TO WIRES AT CENTER

15"

½"

GLUE UP TO DOTTED LINE

CUT TWO

3"

2"

½"

PLAN FOR CARRIAGE STRIPS

7½"

10"

8"

CUT FOUR CARDBOARD DISKS FOR WHEELS

ASSEMBLED CARRIAGE STRIPS

Plate E

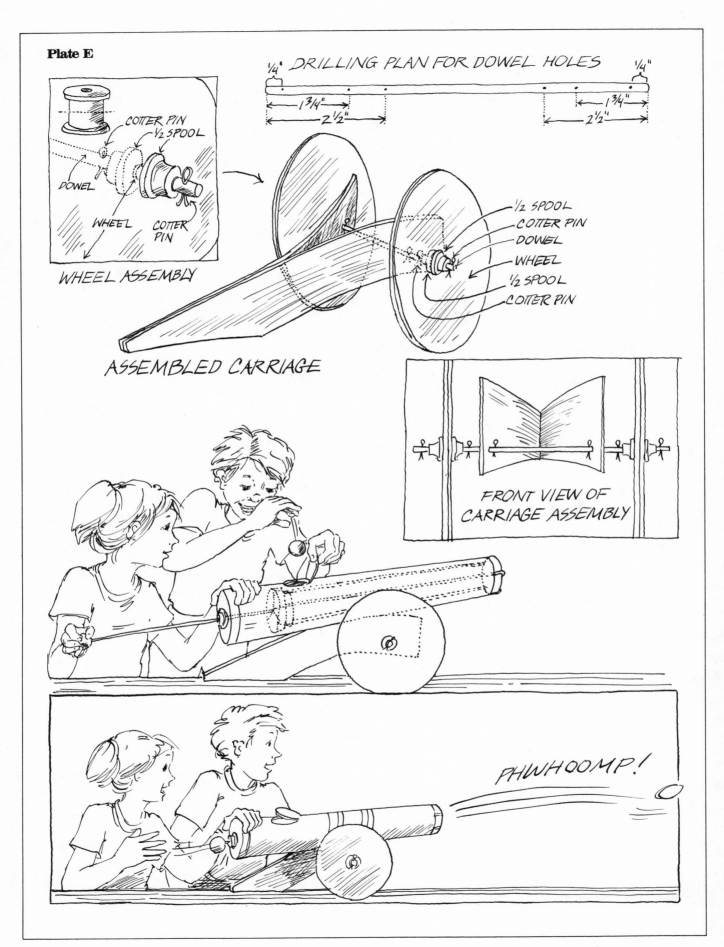

WHEEL ASSEMBLY

COTTER PIN
½ SPOOL
DOWEL
WHEEL
COTTER PIN

DRILLING PLAN FOR DOWEL HOLES
¼"
¼"
1¾"
2½"
1¾"
2½"

ASSEMBLED CARRIAGE

½ SPOOL
COTTER PIN
DOWEL
WHEEL
½ SPOOL
COTTER PIN

FRONT VIEW OF
CARRIAGE ASSEMBLY

PHWHOOMP!

a circle just slightly larger than the circumference of the small end of the barrel. Slip it over the end of the barrel and tape it in place all the way around with gummed tape. This reinforces the barrel end and keeps it circular.

Thread a 30-inch length of strong cotton cord through the hole in the back (larger end) of the barrel and out the open end. Then tie this cord to the wires on the back of the shot thrower where they converge. Pull the end of the cord until the shot thrower is just inside the mouth of the barrel with the rubber bands sticking out. Cut a length of adhesive tape 1 inch longer than the circumference of the barrel mouth. Put the tape through the ends of the rubber bands and tape them to the outside of the barrel mouth. They should be evenly spaced around it. Pull the cord from the back until the shot thrower is inside the barrel with the rubber bands straight but not stretched. Tie a large wooden bead or a half spool to the cord outside the barrel to hold the shot thrower in this position. This completes the shooting mechanism.

To complete the gun carriage, use the point of your scissors and make a 3/8-inch hole on each side of the carriage, where shown in the plan. Drill six 1/8-inch holes in the 8-inch dowel: 1/4 inch, 1 3/4 inches, and 2 1/2 inches in from either end. This makes the axle. Put a cotter pin in the two inside, or center, holes and bend them open. Put the axle through the holes in the carriage. Then put cotter pins through the next two holes, locking the carriage in place. Finish by putting the wheels on and then the last two cotter pins. Tape the finished barrel on top of the gun carriage with several strips of gummed tape. To fire the gun, pull back on the string until the shot thrower cup is behind the loading hole, drop in a Ping-Pong ball, and let go of the string.

This model worked so well that we started to think about bigger and better artillery, and here's a suggestion for the ambitious cannon maker. Use one of the large cardboard tubes that carpets are rolled on for a barrel. Make the shot thrower in the same manner as for the small cannon, but it must be sturdier — substitute shock cord for the rubber bands. Try automotive or boating supply stores for shock cord. We picture a glorious Fourth of July party with two big cannons and a British and Colonial Army bombarding each other with water balloons across a backyard fence.

PART SIX

MYSTERY POWERED TOYS

Secret Sources of Movement

People have always loved to fool the other guy. There is nothing more elevating to the spirits than being in the know while others are standing around looking puzzled. The self-assured Victorians loved mysteries. They were too enlightened to suspect collusion with the devil in magic tricks, but they were still innocent enough to be awed. Most nineteenth-century boys' books included instructions for legerdemain, or sleight-of-hand, as well as how to produce grotesque illusions to startle and amaze your friends. This interest in magic, coupled with a fascination for scientific knowledge, encouraged the development of toys that worked in a mysterious manner. Our little camphor boats that sail around a bowl in such a sprightly fashion seem magical, unless you know the reaction of camphor to water. The weather house design is based on the knowledge that catgut will coil in dry air and unwind in damp air, but disguised as it is, the results seem miraculous.

The bottle imp was another popular mystery toy. Its secret is based on the compressibility of air and water. Street conjurers mystified onlookers with these obedient performers, and household magicians soon learned the trick. The imps are hollow figures with small holes to admit water. When they are placed in a container of water that has an airtight rubber seal, any pressure on the rubber will force water into the figure, making it sink. Variations in pressure will make the imps rise and fall, as if on command. The trick works especially well if you have a good line of patter and nobody notices that you are pressing on the rubber cap.

These whimsical toys were called *ludions* in France and *imps* in England, but in New York, where they were sold on the streets in 1889, they were called *McGintys* after a popular song of the day.

Down went McGinty to the bottom
*   of the sea,*
And he must be very wet,
For they haven't found him yet,
But they say his ghost comes round
*   the docks,*
Before the break of day,
Dressed in his best suit of clothes.

The compressed man was typical of the many macabre illusions that so delighted the Victorians. Grown men as well as boys seem to have indulged in these somewhat disturbing theatrics.

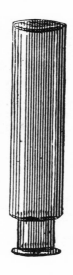

The simplest method of making bottle imps was to decorate medicine vials with painted faces and cloth skirts. The operator was directed to "pretend to mesmerize the little images, not letting it be known that they are bottles, and by some wonderful power you are supposed to possess, can make them obey your slightest wish."

The "dwarf" was another popular illusion. It required two performers, one for the head and legs, the second for the dwarf's arms. "The gestures are apt to be ludicrous, as the second player usually has trouble in fitting his actions to the words of the first. The dwarf can dance and perform many remarkable feats, such as rubbing his head with his toe, or putting both feet in his mouth at once."

PLAN FOR MAKING THE LITTLE WOMAN

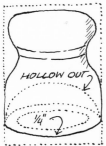

HOLLOW OUT
¼"

BODY
(FULL SCALE)
CARVE FROM
1½" X 1" CORK.
HOLLOW OUT
BOTTOM, LEAVE
¼" BORDER.

HEAD
(FULL SCALE)
CARVE
FROM
¾" X 1"
CORK

HAT
(FULL
SCALE)

(CUT OUT)

ARM
AND
LEG
(FULL SCALE)
CUT TWO
OF EACH

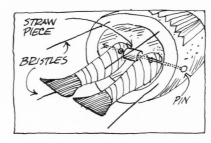

STRAW PIECE

BRISTLES

PIN

PIN   HAT

PIN   PIN

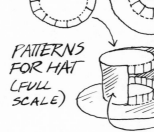

BRISTLE

ASSEMBLED
FIGURES

PLAN FOR MAKING THE LITTLE MAN

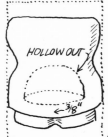

HOLLOW OUT
⅜"

BODY

HEAD
(FOLLOW
PLANS FOR
LITTLE
WOMAN)

PANT LEG
(BOTTOM
OF
JACKET)

PIN

STRAW
PIECE   BRISTLE

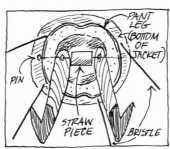

TOP

(CUT OUT)

BRIM

PATTERNS
FOR HAT
(FULL
SCALE)

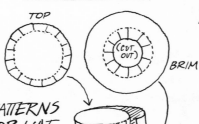

WRAP PAPER AROUND AND
GLUE TO TOP AND BRIM.

PIN

PIN

K-PIN
BUTTONS

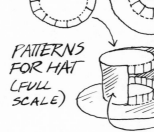

PLAN FOR MAKING THE LITTLE DOG

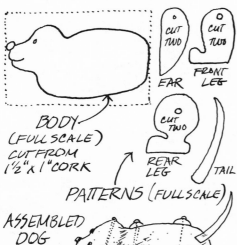

BODY
(FULL SCALE)
CUT FROM
1½" X 1" CORK

CUT TWO
EAR

CUT TWO
FRONT
LEG

CUT TWO
REAR LEG   TAIL

PATTERNS (FULL SCALE)

ASSEMBLED
DOG

PIN

BRISTLE

MUSICAL FIGURES

Musical figures, or bristle dolls, once "hopped with great spirit and originality" when set upon a harpsichord — probably to keep an eighteenth-century girl company while she practiced her scales. They make no sound themselves, but will dance very prettily to someone else's music. If you don't have a harpsichord in your house, put them on any flat vibrating surface: a piano sounding board, a drum, a tin tray you can tap, or even a washing machine that is running. They will move in most unexpected ways.

Tools and Materials

Scissors
Knife: a sharp paring or jackknife
Paintbrushes: small artist's
Paint: artist's acrylic or model
White glue
Pins: straight sewing
Cardboard: lightweight
Tracing paper
Tissue paper
Construction paper
Corks: five corks, 1 1/2 inches by 1 inch
Plastic drinking straws
Bristles: stiff, from a floor scrub brush or a
   hairbrush

To Build Musical Figures

Carve the corks to the sizes shown in the plan. Use one cork for each body and one half cork for each head. The dog is made from a single cork. Keep the figures quite broad and short so they won't topple over easily. Carve out the center of the corks, as shown, leaving about 1/4 inch of cork around the edge. Cut the arms, legs, ears, and a tail of cardboard the size of the patterns. Paint the figures and the cardboard pieces as you choose. Make the hats and the man's trousers and tie of construction paper. The lady's apron and the flower in her hat are tissue paper. She is wearing high-button shoes and striped stockings, which are both painted on.

When all the paint is dry, glue on the heads and attach the legs, arms, and ears with straight pins, as shown. The legs are separated by 1/8-inch pieces cut from a straw. Insert four bristles at even spaces around the bottom of each figure and trim them even. The bristles should be just long enough to allow the legs to swing freely.

CAMPHOR BOATS

This is a traditional toy whose origins are obscure, but chances are good that your great-grandfather played with one. The boats can be as simple as you want to make them, or they can be perfectly accurate models. The main thing to keep in mind is that they must be very lightweight, or they won't work. The designs given here are really cartoons of vintage boats, not realistic models. They are very easy to make.

Tools and Materials

Scissors
Knife: a very sharp paring knife
Paintbrush: fine, pointed watercolor
Sandpaper
Balsa wood: one piece 1 inch by 1 inch by 7 inches
Toothpicks: both round and flat ones
Clear acetate sheet, heavy gauge, 8 inches by 10 inches
Paint: artist's acrylic or model
Clear acrylic finish
Tracing paper
White glue
Tissue paper: white
Camphor (from drug or hardware store)

To Build a Camphor Boat

Pick one of the designs; then using tracing paper, make a pattern and carve the parts from balsa wood; sand them smooth. Smoke-stacks are cut from round toothpicks. Masts are round toothpicks, with flat toothpicks glued on for gaffs and booms. Sails are cut from tissue paper. Assemble the parts and glue them together. Paint the boat carefully. When it dries, paint it again (sails, too, if your boat has them) with clear acrylic finish.

Cut heavy acetate sheeting to the shape of the base pattern and glue the boat to it. Be sure that the boat is on the center line and placed slightly toward the curved front of the base. Fill a clean basin with water. Wedge a small piece of camphor in the notch at the back of the base, and set the boat lightly on the water. Take care that no water comes over the acetate base; it must ride on the surface like a water skipper. As the camphor starts to dissolve, the boats will start to move. If there is any grease at all on the water, the boats won't go, so skim it clean with a piece of newspaper, if necessary.

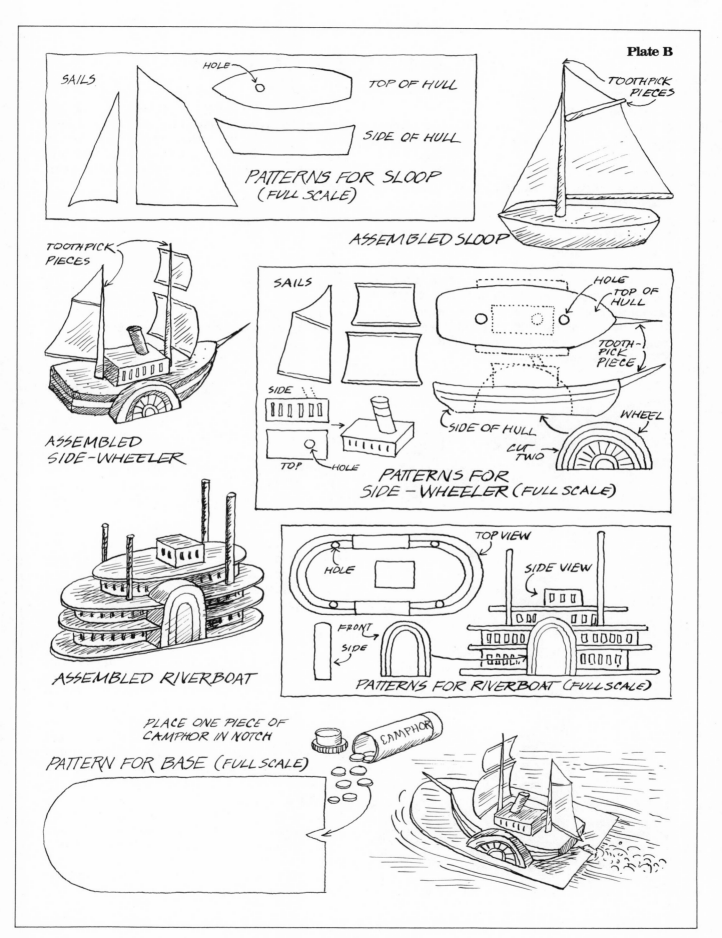

SAILS

HOLE

TOP OF HULL

SIDE OF HULL

PATTERNS FOR SLOOP
(FULL SCALE)

TOOTHPICK PIECES

ASSEMBLED SLOOP

TOOTHPICK PIECES

ASSEMBLED SIDE-WHEELER

SAILS

HOLE
TOP OF HULL

TOOTH-PICK PIECE

SIDE

TOP   HOLE

SIDE OF HULL

WHEEL

CUT TWO

PATTERNS FOR SIDE-WHEELER (FULL SCALE)

ASSEMBLED RIVERBOAT

TOP VIEW

HOLE

SIDE VIEW

FRONT

SIDE

PATTERNS FOR RIVERBOAT (FULL SCALE)

PLACE ONE PIECE OF CAMPHOR IN NOTCH

PATTERN FOR BASE (FULL SCALE)

CAMPHOR

OBEDIENT BALLOON

This, as you can see, is a variation on the Bottle Imp, but the Obedient Balloon is a great deal more decorative and makes an intriguing addition to any room. Ballooning became popular in the late eighteenth century, and an ascension attracted great excitement. The early balloons were very beautiful, often painted with elaborate scenes and hung with bright flags, so just let your imagination go as you are decorating yours.

You might be interested to know that the first live balloon passengers were a duck, a rooster, and a sheep. They all landed safely except for the rooster, whose wing was broken when the sheep kicked him. This ascension took place at Versailles in 1783. King Louis XVI was an enthusiastic spectator. He immediately offered to supply a condemned

criminal as the first human cargo, but De Rozier, the King's historian, gallantly volunteered to make the first trip. He wanted to make history instead of writing about it, and he made a spectacular 25-minute flight over the spires of Paris.

Tools and Materials

Hammer
Needle-nose pliers
Paintbrushes: small artist's
Scissors
Glass jar: 12 inches or more tall with a wide mouth, preferably one that you can fit your hand through
Ping-Pong ball
Metal thimble
Fishing sinkers: split-shot lead — twenty to twenty-five, 3/0 size
Plastic net: one piece 4 3/4 inches by 6 inches, of the kind used to package garlic or flower bulbs
Rubber balloon: a large, strong one
Wide rubber band
A nail
Wire: very fine
Model paint
Florist's clay
HO scale figures: boxed sets of people in nineteenth-century costumes are available at hobby shops

To Make an Obedient Balloon

To make the balloon, punch a small hole, approximately 1/8 inch in diameter in a Ping-Pong ball. Paint the ball with model paint so that it looks like a balloon. Keep in mind as you are decorating it that the hole must be at the bottom of the balloon. You can paint the thimble to look like a gondola too. Cut the plastic net to size. You will notice that the netting stretches more in one direction than it does in the other. Cut it so that the 6-inch length has the least stretch. Wrap the netting around the ball to measure it. The 4 3/4-inch width should be just enough to fit tightly without overlapping. Trim to fit if necessary.

Remove the ball and put a wire around the top and one around the bottom of the net to

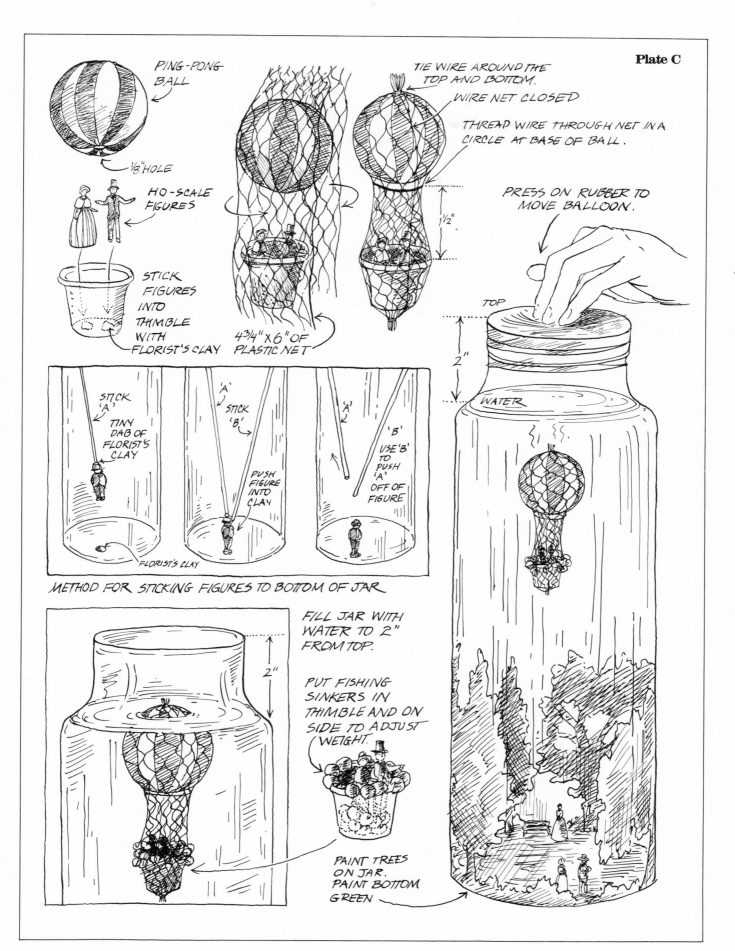

Plate C

PING-PONG BALL

⅛" HOLE

HO-SCALE FIGURES

STICK FIGURES INTO THIMBLE WITH FLORIST'S CLAY

TIE WIRE AROUND THE TOP AND BOTTOM.

WIRE NET CLOSED

THREAD WIRE THROUGH NET IN A CIRCLE AT BASE OF BALL.

½"

4¾" X 6" OF PLASTIC NET

PRESS ON RUBBER TO MOVE BALLOON.

TOP

2"

WATER

STICK 'A'

TINY DAB OF FLORIST'S CLAY

'A'

STICK 'B'

PUSH FIGURE INTO CLAY

FLORIST'S CLAY

'A'

'B'

USE 'B' TO PUSH 'A' OFF OF FIGURE

METHOD FOR STICKING FIGURES TO BOTTOM OF JAR

FILL JAR WITH WATER TO 2" FROM TOP.

PUT FISHING SINKERS IN THIMBLE AND ON SIDE TO ADJUST WEIGHT.

PAINT TREES ON JAR. PAINT BOTTOM GREEN

2"

form a bag, as shown in the drawing. Insert the Ping-Pong ball at the top and run a wire drawstring through the netting just underneath the ball to hold it in place. Put the thimble in at the bottom and wire the netting together around the ball and thimble, leaving a 1 1/2-inch opening in the middle. Stick a small dab of florist's clay in the bottom of the thimble and push two little aeronauts well into the clay. The thimble gondola should be about to their waists. You may think that the men are not dressed properly, but old time balloonists really did go sailing off in their best clothes and top hats.

To decorate the jar, paint the outside of the bottom green. Paint several trees around the sides. You will be able to see the trees both through the glass and on the outside, so look at both views as you paint. You may want to add a few fluffy clouds if your jar is fairly tall. Stick several spectators to the inside bottom of the jar with florist's clay. If the jar has a mouth wide enough for your hand to fit through, this is no problem. But if you cannot get your hand in, you will have to manage the business differently. Drop a small pellet of florist's clay into the bottle and jiggle it into position. Then, using a tiny bit of clay, suspend a figure by its head from the end of a long stick. Move the figure into position and, with a second long stick, push it into the pellet of clay on the bottom and release it from the first stick.

Now you are ready to test the balloon: fill the jar with water to within 2 inches of the top. Put about 15 or 20 sinkers into the thimble with the aeronauts and nip a few around the netting at the edge of the gondola, like sandbags. Gently place the balloon and thimble in the water, making sure that the hole is at the bottom. The balloon should float with its top just at the surface of the water. Add or remove sinkers until it does this. Cut a piece of rubber balloon large enough to stretch over the mouth of the bottle. Fasten it in place with a heavy rubber band. This cover must make an airtight seal. Press down gently on the rubber cover and the balloon will descend; stop pressing and it will rise. By varying the pressure, you control the movement.

HANSEL AND GRETEL WEATHER HOUSE

Weather houses were popular a hundred years ago, and this method of building one is from that period, which might cause a slight problem. You will need a piece of catgut, such as the third string from a violin. We went, in our innocence, to the local violin maker to buy a string and were told that catgut is seldom used any more. Modern synthetics are preferred because they don't stretch in damp weather. Of course, this is the very reason we wanted catgut, because it does. After the lecture, the violin maker produced the very string we needed, so don't you be discouraged if you don't find one on the first try. The Weather House is worth the extra effort. Cat lovers needn't be put off; catgut really comes from sheep. You will probably have good luck if you try a sporting goods store or a place where they restring tennis racquets.

Tools and Materials

Razor knife
Needle-nose pliers
Drill: with 1/8 inch bit
Catgut: about 12 or 15 inches, depending on the size of the box.
Cigar box: or other sturdy box, about 8 inches by 5 inches, by 2 1/2 inches deep
Paintbrush
Plastic berry boxes
Cardboard: heavyweight
Sandpaper: very coarse, sand-colored, two large sheets
Binder paper
Construction paper: black
Acetate film: clear
Pipe cleaners
Facial tissue

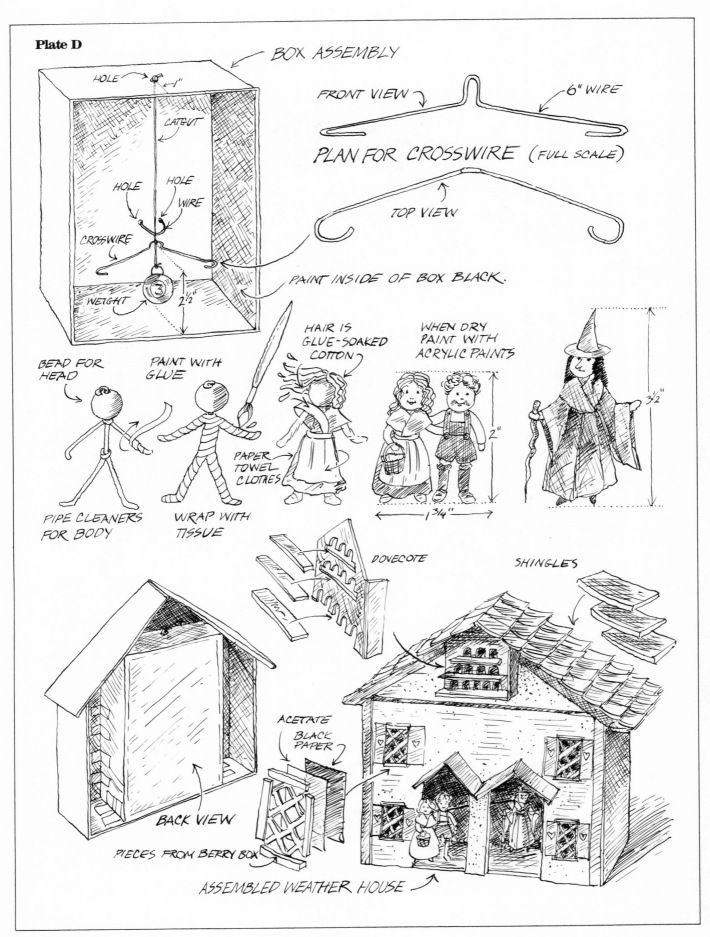

Plate D

BOX ASSEMBLY

HOLE ←1"

CATGUT

FRONT VIEW

6" WIRE

PLAN FOR CROSSWIRE (FULL SCALE)

HOLE   HOLE

WIRE

TOP VIEW

CROSSWIRE

WEIGHT   2½"

PAINT INSIDE OF BOX BLACK.

BEAD FOR HEAD

PAINT WITH GLUE

HAIR IS GLUE-SOAKED COTTON

WHEN DRY PAINT WITH ACRYLIC PAINTS

3½"

PAPER TOWEL CLOTHES

2"

PIPE CLEANERS FOR BODY

WRAP WITH TISSUE

1¾"

DOVECOTE

SHINGLES

ACETATE BLACK PAPER

BACK VIEW

PIECES FROM BERRY BOX

ASSEMBLED WEATHER HOUSE

126

Paper towel
Cotton, absorbent
White glue
Masking tape
Beads: three, 3/8-inch wooden
Wire: 18-gauge, 9 inches
Paints, artist's acrylic
Fishing weight: one, 3-ounce

To Build a Weather House

To make the box, remove the lid and paint the inside of the box black. Drill a hole in the center of one end of the box about 1 inch in from the open side. Thread the catgut through the hole from the inside and knot the end above the hole so it won't slip through. Cut a 6-inch length of 18-gauge wire. Bend it, as shown, and tie it to the catgut about 2 1/2 inches from the bottom of the box. Tie the fishing weight to the end of the catgut so it swings free of the bottom of the box by 1/2 of an inch. Drill two holes in the back of the box just above the suspended crosswire. Bend a small piece of wire through these holes and out and around the catgut to keep it from swinging.

To make the figures, fashion the bodies from pipe cleaners with beads for heads. Hansel and Gretel should be about 2 inches high, and the witch, 3 1/2 inches including her hat. Wrap the pipe cleaners with facial tissue to shape the bodies and paint them with white glue. Hair can be made of absorbent cotton saturated with glue. Dress the figures with bits of paper toweling stuck on with white glue; arrange the folds as they dry. The old witch's hat is made of binder paper, and she has a bent twig for a cane. When the figures are dry, paint them with acrylics. This will soften the glue slightly and allow you to make some final adjustments to their clothes. Glue Hansel and Gretel side by side with their arms around each other so that the two figures together are no wider than 1 3/4 inches.

Now the figures must be attached to the proper side of the crosswire. To determine which side, you will have to experiment. Boil some water in a teakettle and direct some steam into the box. The catgut will start to unwind with the moisture. The end of the wire that swings forward when steamed is where the witch is to be attached; Hansel and Gretel go on the other side. Squeeze the ends of the wire around the necks of the figures to hold them. They must swing free of the bottom of the box and be carefully balanced.

To make the house, cut the front from heavy cardboard. The size will depend on the dimensions of your box. The house is larger than the box. Cut two doorways side by side, just big enough for the figures to come through. Cover the front of the house with a sheet of sandpaper; it will look like stucco. Cut the window frames and mullions from the berry boxes or make them of narrow strips of cardboard. Back the frames with pieces of clear acetate film over black construction paper. The shutters, beams, and dovecote are cut from cardboard. Cut the roof and sides from cardboard; glue and tape them in place. Paint a piece of heavy cardboard light brown with streaks in it; then cut the shingles from this painted board for the roof. They should be rather uneven. Glue them onto the roof, overlapping them like real shingles. Paint the trim on the house. Position the cigar box at the back of the house so that the figures can swing out through the doors. Glue the box in place.

Try the experiment with the teakettle again. Adjust the knotted catgut at the top of the box so the witch comes forward when the box is bathed with steam. That way she will come out on wet, rainy days. Set the box in a sunny window and make sure that Hansel and Gretel come out. The catgut may take a little time to react; it can't respond instantaneously. When the catgut is adjusted, fix it in position at the top of the box with glue and tape.

MANX MANNEQUINS

This cautionary tale appeared in the November issue of *Boy's Own Paper*, London, 1896, showing that truth-in-advertising was as necessary then as it is today. We don't advise you to go into business selling Manx Mannequins, but you could work up a good deal of interest among your friends with tales of this wonderful "new" plaything.

Those mysterious things advertised as the 'Manx Mannequins' you have perhaps heard of; they were described as being actually alive, and were sold in closed boxes with the lids pasted down, which fact alone ought surely to have raised something more than a suspicion on the part of the intending purchaser; but doubtless many a guileless youth and grass-green country maiden were taken in by the carefully worded advertisement, and paid down their money for the thing that was described as being actually alive, and that it would bleed if pricked, was also capable of feeling pain, and was moreover very much

attached to its owner, and all the attention it required was an occasional wash, etc., etc.

Now that is, as far as it goes, quite true, but the description is calculated to mislead, as the boxes supposed to contain the 'mannequin' were shown in court to contain only a small dress and frill, and instructions for the purchaser to adjust it around his hand and make a representation of a face on the back, with the thumb to form the lower lip of the mouth, similar to that shown. . . . doubtless very comical, but of course the whole thing was a sell.

For those who have any ventriloquial power, this arrangement is useful, and may be easily made by sewing a strip of wide elastic A to back of a frill, which will hold it firmly to the hand, at the same time allowing plenty of action for the thumb, which helps to give so much expression to the face while speaking.